Critical Criminological Perspectives

Series Editors
Reece Walters
Faculty of Law
Queensland University of Technology
Brisbane, Queensland, Australia

Deborah H. Drake
Social Policy & Criminology
The Open University
Milton Keynes, UK

The Palgrave Critical Criminological Perspectives book series aims to showcase the importance of critical criminological thinking when examining problems of crime, social harm and criminal and social justice. Critical perspectives have been instrumental in creating new research agendas and areas of criminological interest. By challenging state defined concepts of crime and rejecting positive analyses of criminality, critical criminological approaches continually push the boundaries and scope of criminology, creating new areas of focus and developing new ways of thinking about, and responding to, issues of social concern at local, national and global levels. Recent years have witnessed a flourishing of critical criminological narratives and this series seeks to capture the original and innovative ways that these discourses are engaging with contemporary issues of crime and justice.

More information about this series at
http://www.palgrave.com/series/14932

Elizabeth R. Turner

Public Confidence in Criminal Justice

A History and Critique

palgrave
macmillan

Elizabeth R. Turner
University of Liverpool
Liverpool, UK

Critical Criminological Perspectives
ISBN 978-3-319-67896-2 ISBN 978-3-319-67897-9 (eBook)
https://doi.org/10.1007/978-3-319-67897-9

Library of Congress Control Number: 2017955028

Cover illustration: Détail de la Tour Ei el © nemesis2207/Fotolia.co.uk

Printed on acid-free paper

This Palgrave Macmillan imprint is published by Springer Nature
The registered company is Springer International Publishing AG
The registered company address is: Gewerbestrasse 11, 6330 Cham, Switzerland

For everyone who encouraged me and made me smile whilst I worked on this project, especially Sarah, Megan and Reuben

Preface

July 2000. In a leaked memo,[1] *Prime Minister Tony Blair worries that he, and his government, are perceived as 'somehow out of touch with gut British instincts'. On crime, he says, he is viewed as 'soft'. His proposed response is to formulate a 'tough public message' by announcing an eye-catching initiative 'e.g. locking up street muggers … this should be done soon, and I, personally, should be associated with it'.*

This book is for anyone who is worried about the state of democracy. It is likely to be of particular interest to students and researchers of criminology who are wondering what role their field of inquiry might play in helping to combat the kind of shallow, image-obsessed politics of crime and justice exemplified in the short historical episode recounted above. It is also likely to be of interest to anyone concerned about the adequacy and democratic efficacy of survey-based approaches to capturing 'public opinion'.

These issues were a central focus of mine when, for three years from 2006 to 2009, I was employed as a 'Knowledge Transfer Partnership Associate' (KTP Associate) on a three-year programme of research. The research aimed to provide strategic and practical insights into how criminal justice organisations should approach the requirement that they increase 'public confidence in the criminal justice system'. The final report (Turner et al. 2009) highlighted the failure of existing conceptualisations and measures of public confidence to provide a meaningful way of gauging the extent to which members of the public see the criminal justice system as legitimate and are willing to engage with it. My PhD thesis, which developed alongside my work on the project, used the public confidence agenda as a vehicle for exploring the significance of a term which had become fashionable at the time: 'public criminology'.

In a controversial book, entitled *Public Criminology?*, published whilst I was writing my PhD thesis, two of the UK's leading criminologists argued that 'criminology's public role is most coherently and convincingly described as that of contributing to a better politics of crime and its regulation' (Loader and Sparks 2011, 117). This formulation struck a chord with me at the time, and exploring how researchers might contribute to 'a better politics' has remained one of my primary preoccupations. I have written a number of journal articles and book chapters on this topic (see Turner 2008, 2013, 2014, 2016); however, I often felt, when reflecting on feedback from numerous anonymous reviewers, that producing a longer piece of writing would enable me to make and illustrate my arguments more clearly. And that is what I try to do in this book.

Notes

1. See: https://www.theguardian.com/politics/2000/jul/17/labour.politicalnews1 for full-text of memo.

References

Loader, Ian, and Richard Sparks. 2011. *Public Criminology?* London: Routledge.

Turner, Elizabeth R. 2013. Beyond 'Facts' and 'Values': Rethinking Some Recent Debates about Criminology's Public Role. *British Journal of Criminology* 53 (1): 149–166.

———. 2016. Mass Incarceration and Public Opinion on Crime and Justice: From Democratic Theory to Method and Reality. In *Democratic Theory and Mass Incarceration*, ed. Albert W. Dzur, Ian Loader and Richard Sparks, 213–237. Oxford: Oxford University Press.

Turner, Liz. 2008. Public Confidence in the Criminal Justice System: The Impact of a Dominant National-Level Discourse on Research and Practice. *Crime Prevention and Community Safety: An International Journal* 10 (3): 174–189.

———. 2014. Penal Populism, Deliberative Methods and the Production of 'Public Opinion' on Crime and Punishment. *The Good Society* 23 (1): 87–102.

Turner, Liz, E. Campbell, A. Dale, and R. Graham. 2009. *Creating a Knowledge-base of Public Confidence in the Criminal Justice System: Report 5: Final Report on the Empirical Research.* Newcastle upon Tyne: Newcastle University.

Acknowledgements

This book was made possible in the first instance by my employment on a three-year project funded by the Knowledge Transfer Partnerships programme (KTP006241), and match-funded by the Economic and Social Research Council and the Northumbria Local Criminal Justice Board (£120,000). The Principal Investigator was Prof Elaine Campbell (Newcastle University). Dr Ruth Graham (also Newcastle University) was Co-Investigator and Dr Andy Dale (Business Manager of the Northumbria Local Criminal Justice Board) was the lead from the Non-academic Research Partner. Research leave of one semester provided by my current employer, the University of Liverpool, provided me with the necessary time and space to complete the work on this book.

Aside from these necessary 'official' acknowledgements I am particularly grateful to the following people, all of whom made significant contributions in supporting me to develop the ideas contained in this book. Firstly, Sarah Meyers, who encourages and supports me in everything I do. Secondly, my PhD supervisors Elaine Campbell and Ruth Graham, who consistently pushed and challenged me, introduced me to ideas which have left a lasting impression on my intellectual perspective, and, above all, supported and encouraged me in developing my own ideas. And finally (but by no means least) Dr/Inspector Andy Dale whose patience and flexibility throughout the five years that we worked together were invaluable, as were his helpful hints on writing style and his generosity with biscuits!

In addition to these known contributions are those from people who I may never have met. Over the last several years numerous anonymous reviewers have had sight of different aspects of the work presented here. I have tried, so far as I was able, to take account of their feedback and improve on my argument and I am grateful for the way these reviewers challenged me to do so. It goes without saying, though, that any remaining errors and weaknesses remain all my own.

Contents

List of Tables

CHAPTER 1

Public Confidence in Criminal Justice: What's the Problem?

Abstract Turner sets the idea of public confidence in criminal justice in the context of concerns about 'penal populism'. She notes that criminologists have proposed a number of responses to populism, including protecting criminal justice from political influence, better educating the public to produce more informed opinion, and shifting towards a 'better politics' through dialogue and deliberation. Turner suggests that deliberative methods show the most promise when it comes to making sustainable improvements in the politics of criminal justice policy. However, she argues, the dominance of quantitative, survey-based approaches to understanding 'public opinion', including 'public confidence', poses a substantial barrier to adopting a more deliberative approach. In light of this, she proposes, it is necessary to examine how the survey-based approach became dominant in order to challenge it more effectively.

Keywords Penal populism • Democracy • Public opinion • Deliberative methods • Public confidence in criminal justice

The febrile state of late twentieth-century and early twenty-first-century penal politics fostered increasing cynicism about democratic politics amongst some criminologists (Bosworth 2011; Loader 2008). The temptation to engage in 'populist punitiveness' (Bottoms 1995) or 'penal populism' (Pratt 2007; Roberts et al. 2003) became regarded as an

E.R. Turner, *Public Confidence in Criminal Justice*,
Critical Criminological Perspectives,
https://doi.org/10.1007/978-3-319-67897-9_1

unavoidable aspect of turn-of-the-century politics. Noting the undesirable consequences of this political obsession with crime and criminal justice, some criminologists called for matters of crime and penal policy to be 'insulated' (Loader 2011) from the vicissitudes of electoral competitiveness. In particular, they expressed their dismay that politicians in many countries were either unaware of or willing to ignore evidence that the apparent public demand for harsher punishment was frequently based upon widespread public ignorance of some basic facts about crime and the operation of criminal justice (e.g. see Doob and Roberts 1984, 1988; Hough and Roberts 1998). But, removing questions about how we should respond to crime from the sphere of public political debate and delegating them to 'experts' is incompatible with democracy, which, above all things, is premised on the belief that citizens *should* influence the actions of their governments (Loader and Sparks 2011, 122).

As an alternative to anti-democratic insulation, some have suggested that there should be an increased focus on finding ways to make the public better informed about crime and criminal justice and thus improve their overall confidence that the system is in fact meeting their expectations (e.g. see Roberts et al. 2003). This has been referred to as a 'cognitive deficit model' of the problem (Loader 2011). However, experimental research carried out by the UK Home Office found no evidence that providing materials intended to improve the ability of members of the public to recall 'key facts' about crime and criminal justice could produce substantial and enduring effects on their confidence in the criminal justice system (see Chapman et al. 2002; Salisbury 2004; Singer and Cooper 2008, discussed at greater length in the next chapter). Information alone, then, seems unlikely to prove effective in substantially alleviating the punitive pressures experienced by politicians and governments.

In response to the problems with both the insulation- and education-based responses to the problem of 'penal populism', Loader and Sparks (2012, 33) suggest that '[t]he proper response to the pathologies of contemporary crime politics is to seek to craft a better democratic politics, not to flee from politics altogether' (Loader and Sparks 2012, 33). The solution they propose would require expanding 'institutional spaces' in which 'citizens, practitioners, political actors, and researchers' are all engaged in 'investigating and fashioning solutions to the question of how we regulate and live comfortably with crime risk' (147). In other words, dialogue and *deliberation* have an important role to play in a 'better politics'.

Broadly speaking, the term 'deliberative methods' refers to approaches to opinion research which emphasise the active involvement of research participants in a process of examining and debating 'the facts' of the matter on which their opinion is sought. In recent years, several commentators on criminal justice have identified a range of potential benefits in making greater use of deliberative mechanisms for understanding public opinion. These benefits include fostering a more informed public opinion (see Green 2008), allowing participants to express and transcend the intense emotions which can be generated by crime (Girling et al. 2000; Loader 2011), and bringing participants into contact with a range of lived experiences and perspectives which may be far removed from their own (Dzur 2012). There are also encouraging indications from empirical studies that deliberation can help citizens reach more considered and less punitive positions on the topic of criminal justice (e.g. see Luskin et al. 2002).

Despite these promising signs, insufficient attention has been paid to the social and political conditions which must prevail before such methods can start to challenge punitively oriented penal politics in any meaningful way. In particular, it is necessary to consider the obstacles which have, thus far, prevented them from becoming more influential and providing a viable 'exit strategy' (cf. Bell 2014) from punitive penality. Arguably foremost amongst these obstacles is the more familiar survey-based approach to research which has enjoyed a long period of dominance when it comes to capturing and representing 'public opinion' and which, in England and Wales, in the arena of criminal justice, has particularly emphasised quantitative indicators of 'public confidence in criminal justice'.

In this book I argue that the dominant approach to researching public confidence could, and can, be bettered, and that changing this agenda could play a part in helping to bring about 'a better politics of crime and its regulation' (Loader and Sparks 2011, 117). I challenge the implication (which at times becomes an explicit assertion) that public confidence *has to be* researched in a particular way because of the inherent characteristics it has as a real object which pre-exists the research devised to measure it. I argue that this perspective closes down debate and installs one way of knowing in an unwarranted position of dominance over others.

The question of how and why research on public confidence in criminal justice emerged and developed in the way that it did is no mere methodological matter. What can count as knowledge is contingent upon circumstance, is open to transformation, and has wider social and political effects. Though there may be understandable reasons why the knowledge produced has taken the form it has, there is no necessity in the dominant approach to public confidence, and it is not without its costs. In this book I show that researchers who make claims about 'public confidence' based on survey-based methods took a highly topical and evocative 'lay concept' and worked with it as if it referred unproblematically to some real, pre-existing object. The error, to use Durkheim's words, is this:

> We are so accustomed to use these terms, and they recur so constantly in our conversation, that it seems unnecessary to render their meaning precise. We simply refer to the common notion. (Durkheim 1938, 37)

This book tells a story about how the two words denoting the lay concept—'public confidence'—went on a journey and, in the process, were transformed. The journey sees the two words moving across boundaries between different realms of discourse: from political speeches and newspaper articles, into research reports and academic books and journals. By the point in their journey where this book leaves them, the words have moved beyond their original role as a useful but vague rhetorical token and come to be understood by many as denoting something quite specific and real: a pliable social phenomenon that governments can exhort public sector workers to change, and that researchers can claim to measure reliably.

In telling this story, my primary analytical purpose is to show that this transformation of public confidence was contingent upon other developments, social and political. I argue that the development of a public confidence agenda (in research and in policy) cannot be attributed to the inherent characteristics of a pre-existing, independent, social phenomenon, pure, real, awaiting, and deserving investigation.[1] Neither did the dominant, survey-based approach to researching public confidence (which I will later describe as aggregative, general, atomised, passive—AGAP) become dominant because of its inherent methodological superiority. The public confidence agenda was carved out of the raw materials of historical circumstance and political opportunity and has its own consequences for history and politics.

So, to the story. It began at least 400 years ago. The British Library database of British newspapers and pamphlets from 1600 to 1911 contains almost 25,000 articles, advertisements, letters to the editor, and transcribed speeches which deploy the term 'public confidence'. With considerable regularity and consistency, the term has been used to denote support for persons, actions, organisations, or some other category of thing, from politicians to race horses, stocks, and shares, to the health benefits of cocoa. Yet the authors of these articles, speeches, and adverts never defined public confidence. Rather, they used the words as a rhetorical token, standing in for something which it seems was not to be directly apprehended. Its presence (or absence) could be inferred from the way people behaved: what they bought, how they voted, and whether they protested, rioted, or started a revolution.

The story ends (at least as far as this book is concerned) in the early twenty-first century. In the arena of criminal justice in England and Wales, the idea of 'public confidence' has become more than a vague rhetorical gesture in the direction of maintaining the support of the public. It has come to be spoken of as an objectively real and measurable object around which programmes of research and action can be and have been constructed. Confidence is (like the cognate concept 'fear of crime') regarded as 'something out there in the social world to be decoded by the researcher and deployed by the policymaker' (Lee 2007, 15). By the early 2000s, a public confidence *agenda* emerged, and its legacy continues into the present day. This book seeks to fill in what happened in between the beginning and end points indicated here, and to provide a critical discussion of the impact of the shift and why it matters. The rest of this book is structured as follows.

In Chap. 2, I provide an account of the emergence and evolution of research on public confidence in the criminal justice system in England and Wales, providing a chronological overview of key publications, identifying key characteristics of the dominant approach and demonstrating that things could have been otherwise.

In Chap. 3, I deconstruct the dominant survey-based approach to researching public confidence by identifying the 'grid of specification' into which it organises the stuff of reality and showing how this necessarily 'violates' that reality. I also identify and critique several ways in which proponents of the dominant survey-based approach to public confidence have sought to deny, evade, or conceal the fact that their favoured approach to confidence research rests upon value-based decisions.

In Chaps. 4 and 5, I describe the wider historical context against which the public confidence agenda emerged, identifying those shifts and events that provided 'surfaces of emergence' on which the agenda could gain some traction, and pointing towards those chance openings which the agenda was able to 'hook in' to. These two chapters show that rather than having been constructed around an independent social reality, the public confidence agenda in research and policy took root opportunistically in the spaces afforded by historical, social, and political developments.

In the concluding chapter, Chap. 6, I explore the 'costs to existence' of the dominant survey-based approach to public confidence. I argue that surveys impose severe limits on what citizens can 'say', subjecting them to the logic of the research method, and hailing them as individualised consumers. This affects both the operation of the extant political sphere and the way citizens think about themselves and their rights and responsibilities. As such, where they dominate knowledge production through claims to be uniquely able to access an implicitly singular pre-existing 'reality', surveys impede efforts to create a 'better politics'. Ultimately, researchers are involved in the making of political worlds, and this imposes broader ethical responsibilities upon them, which they should not seek to avoid by hiding behind claims to be simply representing an objective reality.

Notes

1. I agree with Law (2004) about the need to contest what he refers to as the 'Euro-American' common-sense assumptions about reality.

References

Bell, Emma. 2014. There Is an Alternative: Challenging the Logic of Neoliberal Penality. *Theoretical Criminology* 18 (4): 489–505.

Bosworth, Mary. 2011. Penal Moderation in the United States? Yes We Can. *Criminology & Public Policy* 10 (2): 335–343.

Bottoms, Anthony. 1995. The Philosophy and Politics of Punishment and Sentencing. In *The Politics of Sentencing Reform*, ed. Chris Clarkson and Rod Morgan, 17–49. Oxford: Clarendon.

Chapman, Becca, Catriona Mirrlees-Black, and Claire Brawn. 2002. *Improving Public Attitudes to the Criminal Justice System: The Impact of Information*. London: Home Office.

Doob, Anthony N., and Julian V. Roberts. 1984. Social Psychology, Social Attitudes, and Attitudes Towards Sentencing. *Canadian Journal of Behavioural Science* 16 (4): 269–280.

———. 1988. Public Punitiveness and Public Knowledge of the Facts: Some Canadian Surveys. In *Public Attitudes to Sentencing: Surveys from Five Countries*, ed. N. Walker and M. Hough, 111–133. Aldershot: Gower.

Durkheim, Emile. 1938. *The Rules of Sociological Method*. New York: The Free Press.

Dzur, A. 2012. *Punishment, Participatory Democracy and the Jury*. Oxford: Oxford University Press.

Girling, Evi, Ian Loader, and Richard Sparks. 2000. *Crime and Social Change in Middle England*. London: Routledge.

Green, David A. 2008. *When Children Kill Children: Penal Populism and Political Culture*. Oxford: Oxford University Press.

Hough, Mike, and Julian V. Roberts. 1998. *Attitudes to Punishment: Findings from the British Crime Survey*. London: Home Office.

Law, John. 2004. *After Method: Mess in Social Science Research*. Abingdon: Routledge.

Lee, Murray. 2007. *Inventing Fear of Crime: Criminology and the Politics of Anxiety*. Cullompton: Willan.

Loader, Ian. 2008. The Anti-politics of Crime. *Theoretical Criminology* 12 (3): 399–410.

———. 2011. Playing with Fire? Democracy and the Emotions of Crime and Punishment. In *Emotions, Crime and Justice*, ed. Susanne Karstedt, Ian Loader, and Heather Strang, 347–362. Oxford: Hart.

Loader, Ian, and Richard Sparks. 2011. *Public Criminology?* London: Routledge.

———. 2012. Beyond Lamentation: Towards a Democratic Egalitarian Politics of Crime and Justice. In *Policing: Politics, Culture and Control*, ed. T. Newburn and J. Peay, 11–42. Oxford: Hart Publishing.

Luskin, Robert C., James S. Fishkin, and Roger Jowell. 2002. Considered Opinions: Deliberative Polling in Britain. *British Journal of Political Science* 32: 455–487.

Pratt, J. 2007. *Penal Populism*. Abingdon: Routledge.

Roberts, Julian V., Loretta J. Stalans, David Indermaur, and Mike Hough. 2003. *Penal Populism and Public Opinion: Lessons from Five Countries*. Oxford: Oxford University Press.

Salisbury, Heather. 2004. *Public Attitudes to the Criminal Justice System: The Impact of Providing Information to British Crime Survey Respondents*. London: Home Office.

Singer, Lawrence, and Suzanne Cooper. 2008. *Inform, Persuade and Remind: An Evaluation of a Project to Improve Public Confidence in the Criminal Justice System*. London: Ministry of Justice.

CHAPTER 2

Constructing Public Confidence: A Chronology of the Research Agenda

Abstract Turner describes the emergence and development of the public confidence research agenda. During the 1970s and 1980s, researchers criticised general measures of public opinion, and proposed the use of specific scenario-based questions in order to gauge opinions about appropriate sentencing practice. However, some researchers suggested that specific measures were artificial, and only general measures could capture 'real life'. During the early 2000s, a dominant understanding of public confidence emerged, which saw it as a real and measurable phenomenon, pre-existing research, and with identifiable causes. Survey-based approaches were promoted as the *only* way to measure true confidence. These approaches are *aggregative* and *general*, premised on an *atomised*, *passive* conception of the citizen (or AGAP). Recalling the doubts about the AGAP approach expressed in the 1970s and 1980s, Turner challenges this dominant view. She argues that proponents of AGAP approaches misrepresent a value-based decision about how to know about confidence.

Keywords Penal populism • Public opinion • Public confidence in criminal justice • British Crime Survey • New Labour • Performance measurement • Quasi-experimental research

E.R. Turner, *Public Confidence in Criminal Justice*,
Critical Criminological Perspectives,
https://doi.org/10.1007/978-3-319-67897-9_2

In the early 1980s, the newly established British Crime Survey (BCS) was promoted by Home Office researchers as a means 'to gauge public confidence' (Hough and Mayhew 1985, 43). By the late 1990s, the data it provided on the proportion of the population identifying as 'fairly confident' or 'very confident' in the criminal justice system played a central part in the performance measurement framework for criminal justice agencies. Confidence was regarded as the most important aspect of public opinion in this policy area. Correspondingly, the first decade of the twenty-first century saw a proliferation of studies of public confidence in the criminal justice system, or parts of the system.

This chapter adopts a chronological approach to chart the evolution of research on public opinion about crime and criminal justice from the late 1970s until 2010. To identify the sample for analysis, I compiled a database of articles, reports, and policy documents which referred directly to either public confidence in the criminal justice system or public confidence in policing.[1] I then examined the references cited in each of these documents in order to identify any other sources which were referenced by more than one of the pieces on confidence. Documents were selected for further analysis if at least one of the following criteria was satisfied: (1) the document had been referenced three or more times in other documents dealing with public confidence; (2) the document was produced by authors who had been referenced three or more times in other documents dealing with public confidence; (3) the document was clearly positioned within the policy agenda as what Foucault called 'prescriptive and programmatic' (O'Farrell 2005, 77), which is to say the document's authors located their work within the context of a body of work implied to be evolving in an orderly and cumulative fashion.

Using examples from the texts analysed, I show how a particular conception of public confidence was constructed and came to dominate. Understood as an aspect of public opinion more generally, public confidence was constructed as a *real* and *measurable* thing, *pre-existing* the research used to capture it, and *caused by* other factors that, it was suggested, could also be identified through the collation of quantitative data.

Quantitative data on public opinion emanates from a number of sources, from polls in newspapers and social media, to commercial polling organisations, to researchers working in or on behalf of government and universities. Whilst there are certainly some significant differences between these different sources (not least in terms of the robustness and sophistication of their methods), their approaches share some basic characteristics. They

- are based on the *aggregation* of individual views;
- are usually (especially in terms of their 'headline' questions) focused on *general* matters (e.g. the criminal justice system, or 'sentencing', or 'the police') rather than specific matters (e.g. specific cases);
- are premised on a conception of the public as comprised of *atomised* individuals who already hold (and are entitled to hold) their own 'personal' opinions or attitudes; and
- only engage participants in a *passive*, non-interactive way, by requiring them to give an on-the-spot evaluation with their responses limited to specific predetermined options.

I refer to knowledge about public opinion produced in this way as aggregative, general, atomised, passive, or AGAP.[2] Knowledge produced through the AGAP approach has dominated political understandings of public opinion about crime and criminal justice over the last 30 years, and 'confidence in the criminal justice system' has consistently been amongst the most prominent of these measures.[3] By conducting a chronological examination of how this research agenda unfolded and developed, we can see moments where alternate perspectives and subtle excesses in analytical interpretation and subsequent representation have been smoothed over, creating a misleading impression of a cumulative and objective body of knowledge.

2.1 1970s: Two Perspectives on Public Opinion about Crime and Justice

In 1978, presenters at the Council of Europe Thirteenth Criminological Research Conference (entitled 'Public Opinion on Crime and Criminal Justice') expressed concern about research purporting to 'capture' public opinion. French sociologist Philippe Robert (1978, 45) observed that claims made about public opinion were 'frequently ill-founded' and that 'badly conducted surveys merely lend these assertions a pseudo-scientific colouring, reinforcing their apparent plausibility.' Sometimes, he suggested, they 'even help to fabricate the "facts" which they claim to reveal'. Along with German criminologist Hans Joachim Schneider, Robert spoke of a worrying tendency to treat public opinion as a single unified phenomenon rather than as a varied, pluralistic one (Robert 1978, 55; Schneider 1978, 121–2). Schneider argued that '[w]e should, as scholars, keep in mind that there is more in public opinion than what the scarcity and simplicity of our present empirical research methods and results can produce'

(Schneider 1978, 122). British criminologist Paul Rock shared their scepticism, arguing that the phenomenon of 'public opinion' is entirely socially constructed through a process whereby complex and fluid everyday thought is pressed into the mould of 'organizational instruments which emphasise logicality and lucidity' and give everyday ideas 'alien meaning' (Rock 1979, 163; 166).

Speaking at the same conference, Dutch criminologist Jan van Dijk cited findings from a public survey carried out in England in 1966 as part of the aborted Royal Commission on the Penal System.[4] This survey found that most members of the public did not have an accurate appreciation of the relative and total incidence of different types of crime recorded each year and that they had very limited levels of knowledge about court procedures and the experience of prison inmates (Banks et al. 1975, 230–235). Based on this, Van Dijk argued that governments should be taking a much more active role in 'publicising the data on the actual crime situation' by supplying media outlets with 'objective information' about crime, including contextual information about the prevalence and 'social correlates' of different types of criminal behaviour, and 'actual victimisation risk' (Van Dijk 1979, 9). Van Dijk's focus, then, was very much on deficiencies in public knowledge about crime and criminal justice which were detrimental to their feelings of safety and their attitudes towards the criminal justice system. In this perspective, opinions are treated as real things, amenable to capture and representation and capable of being remoulded so that they take on more socially beneficial forms.

In the proceedings of this conference, we see the outlines of two different perspectives on how criminologists, and policymakers, ought to respond to apparently worrying trends in public opinion towards criminal justice. One view is that the mechanisms used to measure these opinions are inherently deficient, producing what they purport to represent, and reducing the complexity of public beliefs and sentiments so that what is understood about those beliefs and sentiments is far removed from their messy origins. The other view implies that opinions have a reality that is independent of and pre-exists the research mechanisms, and that these opinions can be moulded by educating the public about the reality of the thing they are being asked to evaluate. The differences between these two perspectives reflect some quite fundamental epistemological and ontological divides. However, as will become clear, these divisions have been obscured by the ascendance of a dominant approach to researching public confidence. It was not, however, inevitable that one perspective would win out over the other. Research conducted during the 1980s reveals an important debate about how to conceptualise, comprehend, and capture public opinion about criminal justice.

2.2 1980s: 'False Shadows' and 'True Substances'

The idea that the public lacked accurate knowledge of the state of crime and criminal justice (highlighted by Van Dijk (1979) and long-suspected by criminal justice professionals and criminologists) was influential in public attitudes research carried out during the 1980s. During that decade, a growing body of research findings established the paucity of public knowledge about crime and criminal justice, suggesting, for example, that members of the British public had a 'distorted view of the sort of offender filling up our prisons' (Shaw 1982, 13) and tended to 'overestimate the leniency of the courts' (Hough and Moxon 1985, 164).

Canadian researchers came to similar conclusions. Their survey respondents overestimated both the proportion of crimes that were violent and rates of reoffending by convicted criminals, most believed that the murder rate had increased since the abolition of the death penalty, and they also lacked accurate knowledge about sentencing policy (statutory minimums and maximums) and actual penalties imposed (Doob and Roberts 1988, 115–116). Researchers in Canada also experimented with asking respondents to evaluate sentences in *specific cases*, showing some respondents media coverage of the case and others the information available to the courts. They found that 'the same sentence was evaluated differently according to the actual account that was read' (Doob and Roberts 1984, 276) and concluded that 'public attitudes to sentencing are shaped not by the reality which takes place in courts, but by the news media.' As a result, they said, 'policy makers should not interpret the public's apparent desire for harsher penalties at face value; they should understand this widespread perception of leniency is founded upon incomplete and frequently inaccurate news accounts' (277).

Back in the UK, Home Office researchers argued that their analysis of the data from the first British Crime Survey, which had, like the Canadian studies, asked respondents to consider some specific sentencing scenarios, offered 'a corrective to widely held misconceptions about popular attitudes to punishment' (Hough and Moxon 1985, 171) because it suggested 'that sentencing practice is broadly in step with public opinion' (Hough and Moxon 1985, 167). In this report, general opinion poll–style questions were criticised as 'insufficiently precise to answer whether sentencing is in line with public opinion—that is, whether people would see court sentences as fair' (Hough and Moxon 1985, 162), and policymakers were enjoined to treat findings from opinion polls which indicated that 'people generally favour a tougher approach' with extreme care (Hough and Mayhew 1985, 43). Researchers argued that specific cases should be used to elicit respondents' sentencing preferences as an alternative to capturing general opinions that were inevitably based on public misperceptions.

The research conducted in the 1980s, including by the Home Office's own researchers, led some to suggest that the inadequacies of public knowledge completely undermined the value of measuring public opinion about the criminal justice system in general: 'Questions designed to find out whether offenders are generally thought to get their just deserts can only be sensibly asked if people hold accurate beliefs about current practice' (Hough and Moxon 1985, 162). Roberts and Doob (1989) argued that 'interpreting opinion polls to mean that the public are greatly dissatisfied with the severity of current sentencing practice is, in Shakespeare's words, to take "false shadows for true substances"' (Roberts and Doob 1989, 515). However, although there was clear evidence that general measures of public opinion provided findings that were ripe for political misinterpretation, during the 1990s an alternative perspective became dominant.

2.3 1990s: Real, Measurable, and Caused

> Specificity is important ... if people's views are to be elicited about the appropriateness of sentences; but this does not entitle us to ignore the results of unspecific questions about sentencing policy. They may be measuring something which specific questions do not: a generalized satisfaction or – more often – dissatisfaction with what respondents vaguely believe to be official sentencing policy. (Walker and Hough 1988, 8)

Research indicating that members of the public were frequently ill-informed about matters of crime and criminal justice and, when asked to propose sentences for specific scenarios, were less punitive than had been assumed was used by some to argue that general measures of opinion should be treated with care, or not used at all. However, the quotation from Walker and Hough (above) suggests an alternative perspective. For them, the distinction between the specific and general indicators of opinion is not a matter of them revealing 'true substances' and 'false shadows' (as Roberts and Doob [1989] had argued). Rather it is that they capture distinctive, but *equally valuable*, phenomena. This view justifies the continued use of general measures of opinion despite their much-discussed limitations.

So, signs from the 1980s that Home Office researchers would shun general opinion measures were misleading. And the more critical and reflexive points raised at the Council of Europe conference by Robert, Schneider, and Rock (that surveys may produce the facts they purport to represent, that they impose 'alien meaning', that public opinion is a social construct) were smoothed over. It was Van Dijk's proposals about the need to educate the public such that their opinions would be better informed that eventually exerted the most influence. Van Dijk is referenced in the report on the first BCS (Hough and Mayhew 1983) and even receives an expression of gratitude from the authors. Walker and Hough's (1988) assertion about the value of measures of 'generalized satisfaction' (see above) proved prophetic for the direction taken by research on public opinion in relation to crime and criminal justice. During the 1990s, measures of public opinion, and especially of public confidence, assumed ever greater prominence in the UK context.

The 1996 BCS included a new suite of questions on public attitudes and knowledge. The report on the findings these indicators generated (Hough and Roberts 1998) appears to have precipitated two subtle but important shifts in the way in which research into public opinion on issues of crime and justice was framed. Firstly, the report specifically linked public attitudes on sentencing to the 'need to sustain public confidence', thus tying together empirical research and the idea of public confidence in the criminal justice system which, as will be discussed later, became politically prominent during the 1980s and 1990s. Secondly, it positioned public confidence and public knowledge within a causal schema. Yet the report as a whole did not depart dramatically from the cautious approach adopted during the 1980s. What was different (as will be discussed further in Chap. 5) was the political context into which its findings were released. This context meant that only certain aspects of the report were picked up on by policymakers, whilst others were ignored. Inadvertently, Hough and Roberts influenced the design of a blueprint for researching public confidence. The parts of their report which may have troubled this blueprint were largely ignored.

Referring directly to the research done in the 1980s, Hough and Roberts (1998) reiterated the point that 'the public were less punitive than was generally supposed' (2). They also repeated the argument that low levels of public knowledge about crime and criminal justice necessitated a sophisticated methodological approach to be able to access 'true' preferences. Their analytical approach and conclusions were very like the studies from the 1980s. For example, analysing the data from a question which asked about people's sentencing preferences in a case of burglary they found that the responses were generally more lenient than magistrates' guidelines. They also found that respondents tended to think that the case they had been given to 'sentence' was a low-level scenario. They suggested that this latter finding

> underscores how *useless for policy* it is to provide survey findings pitched at a general level. If the general public overestimates the seriousness of the average burglary, as appears to be the case here, those responsible for sentencing policy can derive little of value from the finding that, on average, people think that 80 per cent of burglars should be locked up. (28, emphasis added)

However, this aspect of their analysis was far less influential than claims made very early in the report:

> The 1996 BCS suggests that there is a *crisis of confidence* in sentencers which needs tackling with some urgency ... People think that sentencers are out of touch, and that their sentences are too soft. ... Correcting public misperceptions about sentencing trends in this country should promote greater public confidence in judges and magistrates. And since the judiciary occupy such a critical place in the criminal justice system, increasing confidence in the courts should promote confidence in the administration of justice. (x, emphasis added)

They went on to state:

> The public are dissatisfied with sentencing practice, or what they perceive sentencing practice to be. What is responsible for this dissatisfaction? One explanation is that people simply do not have an accurate perception of the sentencing process. Recent qualitative work employing focus groups (Hough, 1996) has uncovered systematic ignorance of current sentencing patterns, and has demonstrated that this is a factor fuelling public dissatisfaction with the courts. (2, emphasis added)

Two important points from this report proved influential for subsequent policy. Firstly, the identification of a 'crisis of confidence', and secondly the clear identification of a plausible solution: 'correcting public misperceptions'. The report provides reassurance for policymakers by offering 'to chart opinion in an authoritative way and to explore the factors which shape this opinion' (3). Crucially, rather than labouring the point that poor public knowledge is a reason for policymakers to avoid paying too much attention to general measures of dissatisfaction, this report repositioned poor public knowledge as a *causal factor* in public dissatisfaction with sentencing, and thus in low levels of public confidence in the criminal justice system as a whole.

In this report, then, the dominant framing of the problem of public confidence appeared highly sympathetic to an obvious cause of frustration for policymakers: the multiple manifestations of public opinion they are exposed to which are of varying reliability and seemingly profoundly influenced by the media, particularly the tabloid newspapers. Hough and Roberts represented researchers like themselves as being on hand to offer a solution, claiming that 'these conduits of public opinion can provide a distorted image of public views. *The only truly valid measure of opinion is a representative survey.*' (1, emphasis added). By cross-tabulating 'beliefs about leniency' with 'estimated use of imprisonment' they showed that 'people who are dissatisfied with the severity of sentences are also those who are particularly inaccurate' (21). This, they claimed, 'suggests that ignorance about current practice is one source of public dissatisfaction with sentencing' (21). They also found that '[p]eople who thought that crime was steeply on the increase were more likely than others to think that sentences were too lenient' (21).

In their conclusion, Hough and Roberts argued that it was 'important to educate the public about trends in crime and the proportion of crime that involves violence' (43).[5] This manner of response to 'crisis' appealed to civil servants and politicians, as well as criminologists and other scholars concerned with halting the apparent trend towards what had been dubbed 'populist punitiveness' (Bottoms 1995). The techniques for education which Hough and Roberts (1998) proposed included exploiting 'the communication techniques of the late twentieth century' to ensure that people were made aware of key facts and 'identify[ing] key audiences ... and convey[ing] in media appropriate to each audience an accurate portrayal of current sentencing practice' (45). This approach must have seemed reassuringly compatible with the political practices credited with enabling Labour's landslide election win of 1997: a campaign of tactically targeted communications and rebranding.

This 1998 report functioned in many ways as the blueprint for the subsequent development of research and policy around public confidence in the criminal justice system. Its enduring contribution has been to cement an understanding amongst policymakers and criminal justice practitioners of confidence as something which is real, measurable, and caused by other factors (viz. poor public knowledge) and thus amenable to correction. Although the report did repeat the earlier warnings about the perils of reading too much into general measures of public opinion, as we shall see this aspect was not much emphasised in subsequent public confidence research.

2.4 2000s: Consolidation of an Agenda

In the late 1990s, the Labour government adopted promoting public confidence in the criminal justice system as an explicit objective and set quantitative performance targets to be measured through the BCS (see Mattinson and Mirrlees-Black 2000, 47–48). There followed an expansion in the amount of attention which the specific concept of 'public confidence in the criminal justice system' received from researchers and a substantial increase in the volume of available analysis emanating both from the BCS and from commissioned research studies with confidence as their focus. From 1998 onwards, analysis of public confidence in the criminal justice system became a routine component of the BCS work programme and was conducted very much along the lines of the blueprint developed based on Hough and Roberts (1998), whose report was frequently cited.

Mattinson and Mirrlees-Black (2000) drew their readers' attention to the fact that Hough and Robert's (1998) report had 'led to increasing awareness of the importance of educating the public about crime and criminal justice' (Mattinson and Mirrlees-Black 2000, 2), and noted that the Home Office had subsequently engaged in discussions with criminal justice partners about suitable initiatives to achieve this aim. Comparing the figures from the 1998 BCS to those from 1996 Mattinson and Mirrlees-Black arrived at the encouraging inference that 'there was some evidence that the message of falling crime was getting across to the public' as the percentage of respondents believing that crime was rising fell from 75% in 1996 to 59% (3), nonetheless the public still 'overestimate the crime problem' (4).

A new set of questions on perceptions of juvenile offending included in the 1998 BCS identified what Mattinson and Mirrlees-Black referred to as a 'great disparity between perceptions and the statistics' most likely caused by 'media portrayals of persistent juvenile offenders and the continuing influence of the James Bulger murder on the public psyche' (14). Their analysis confirmed the existence of 'a relationship between low levels of knowledge and negative assessments of juvenile justice' (22). They also argued that '[t]o target strategies to tackle misperceptions about juvenile crime effectively, it is necessary to identify those with the poorest knowledge' (15). Mattinson and Mirrlees-Black explicitly positioned their analysis and report as 'updating' the work done by Hough and Roberts (1998) and were careful to note the continuity between their work (on knowledge of juvenile offending and justice) and the work undertaken by Hough and Roberts (which focused on adult offending): 'we can only draw the same conclusion as Hough and Roberts—correcting public misperceptions of juvenile crime should promote greater public confidence in juvenile courts' (Mattinson and Mirrlees-Black 2000, 45).

The emphasis placed on continuity with Hough and Roberts (1998) in subsequent reports clearly shows their influence, as well as suggesting a more general concern with elaborating a continuous, cumulative body of knowledge. However, this surface appearance of continuity conceals a tendency to mis- or over-interpret the significance of earlier studies. For example, Mattinson and Mirrlees-Black suggested that Hough and Roberts (1998) had argued that 'there was a public crisis of confidence in the criminal justice system (CJS)' and that 'very low opinions of the courts and sentencers ... were undermining public confidence in the criminal justice system' (Mattinson and Mirrlees-Black 2000, 47). These statements go beyond the claims made by Hough and Roberts, which were that there was a 'crisis of confidence in *sentencers*' and that, due to their centrality within the criminal justice system increasing confidence in the judiciary and the courts '*should* promote confidence in the administration of justice' (Hough and Roberts 1998, x, emphasis added). These minor over-interpretations of Hough and Roberts (1998) make their conclusions appear significantly more categorical than they probably intended. Through such episodes of subtle mis- or over-interpretation, over time knowledge about public confidence has been discursively constructed as an altogether more concrete and certain affair than was indicated in some of the earlier studies.

That the relationship between knowledge and confidence is *causal* (the central theme from Hough and Roberts [1998]) underpinned successive analyses of the BCS after 1998, and each successive 'sweep' of analysis tended to reference (if not reproduce verbatim) excerpts from previous years, so, for example:

> Giving people access to accurate information about crime and the criminal justice system is essential to securing confidence in the system. Previous sweeps of the BCS (Hough and Roberts 1998; Mattinson and Mirrlees-Black 2000) have shown that .... (Mirrlees-Black 2001, 5)

> Giving people access to accurate information about crime and the criminal justice system is essential to securing confidence in the system. Previous sweeps of the BCS (Hough and Roberts 1998; Mattinson and Mirrlees-Black 2000 and Mirrlees-Black 2001) have shown that .... (Whitehead and Taylor 2003, 124)

> There is evidence from previous years of the BCS which suggests that people who are better informed about crime and the criminal justice system tend to rate the system more highly (Mattinson and Mirrlees-Black 2000 and Mirrlees-Black 2001). (Allen et al. 2005, 7)

Meanwhile, Mike Hough and Julian Roberts authored, co-authored or edited several more academic publications during the early 2000s, which referred readers between their different publications creating the sense of a mutually reinforcing knowledge base with considerable intellectual weight behind it (see Roberts and Hough 2002; Hough 2003; Roberts et al. 2003; Roberts and Hough 2005a, b, c).

Further research into public confidence was also commissioned and carried out on both a local and a national basis during the mid-2000s, by which stage a dominant way of doing confidence research had emerged. This dominant approach can be summarised as follows: (1) identify the issues of importance to the public in relation to the CJS (their expectations or what they need to believe or have confidence in); (2) understand how different groups form their opinions on these issues (how they come to know about the CJS in order to be able to believe or not believe); (3) apply knowledge of the above to 'correct' opinions (by providing evidence that the CJS is meeting their expectations)[6]. Thus, the parameters of confidence research were set in such a way that identifying the 'drivers' of confidence, in a style akin to market research, seems to have been regarded by many researchers as their basic task[7]. As such, the analytical focus of many of the studies (e.g. on 'key audiences') appears to reflect pre-existing beliefs about the most appropriate tactics to 'tackle' the problem of low confidence, namely factual education via targeted marketing, a rather good example of what Matthews (2009, 343) has called 'policy driven evidence rather than evidence driven policy'. The methods used in the studies, particularly the focus on techniques of quantitative analysis that seek to identify statistical associations, reinforce the sense of public confidence as real, measurable, and caused by other factors.

This understanding of what confidence research should be about was taken to its logical extreme in several pieces of research adopting quasi-experimental approaches to investigate the relative effectiveness of different techniques for informing the public (see Chapman et al. 2002; Salisbury 2004; Singer and Cooper 2008).[8] As well as referencing and building upon each other and upon the preceding analysis of the BCS, these studies have each been referenced in subsequent research and analysis (see, e.g. Whitehead and Taylor 2003, 124; Allen et al. 2005, 7; Duffy et al. 2007). This cross-referencing between studies reinforces the impression of the body of knowledge on public confidence as cumulative and coherent. Furthermore, the implicit acceptance of these quasi-experimental approaches into the corpus of knowledge underlines the assumption that a causal relationship exists between accurate knowledge (or 'recall') of 'facts' about crime and criminal justice and public confidence in the criminal justice system (which is also assumed to be both real and measurable).

Towards the end of the 2000s, a further two high-profile reports on public confidence were published. The first, another report by Ipsos MORI (Duffy et al. 2007), featured a glowing foreword by one of the key figures in establishing the confidence research agenda, Professor Mike Hough: 'This is an important report and Ipsos MORI is to be congratulated for producing it ... I welcome the report's recommendations ... the report is right to emphasise the need for robust measurement and monitoring of perceptions of crime.' What is most striking about this report is that it purports to write about a serious social problem, one which it alleges has significant ramifications for 'citizens' overall quality of life' (11), but it is clearly aimed at meeting the strategic needs of a *party-political* audience, namely the governing Labour party: the lack of confidence which the British public have in their government's ability to 'crack down on crime and violence' is described as 'a key issue for the government because there is a strong correlation between trends in ratings of performance on crime and trends in voting intention' (3).

The politically partisan nature of the report need not be an issue; companies like Ipsos MORI are relied on by political parties to help plan their election strategies. However, this report was endorsed by a former Home Office researcher–turned academic, who was a key architect in establishing the public confidence agenda as a matter of *national*, not *party-political*, import. It also drew quite heavily on previous research, including research carried out by the Home Office, and explicitly located itself within the context of supposedly non-partisan government reviews being carried out by Louise Casey (2008) (see below) and Sir Ronnie Flanagan (2008). Considering this we should perhaps not be surprised that the report, despite its party-political orientation, attracted the attention of practitioners within criminal justice agencies as the latest piece of 'evidence' about public confidence[9].

The content of the MORI report reprised the by-now-familiar refrain about the public being ill-informed about crime and failing to recognise that crime had fallen. It also offered hope to politicians and practitioners by offering to 'unpick [...] what actually drives the general public's views of crime and the government's handling of it' (Duffy et al. 2007, 11). Arguing that 'public confidence and reassurance are key outcomes in their own right' (59), the report recommended more and better measurement of public perceptions as a way of improving performance, more independent reviews of criminal justice system performance to produce data that the public would be more likely to trust, and that the police should publish more, and better-targeted, information about local issues and how the criminal justice system and its partners are working to tackle them.

As already noted, and despite its clear party-political purposes, the evidence provided by Ipsos MORI received attention within the criminal justice system. It was also referenced in the 2008 report published under the auspices of the Cabinet Office's Crime and Communities Review and led by the high-profile (and controversial) civil servant Louise Casey. The Casey Review (2008) (or *Engaging Communities in Fighting Crime* to give its official title) began with a typically robust assertion by Casey:

> There is a sense that the public can't be trusted to take a view on their policing and Criminal Justice System. During this review I have tried to redress that balance by putting at its heart the voice of the public ... I would urge policy makers, professionals, lobby groups and law makers to take note of one thing - the public are not daft. They know what's wrong, they know what's right, and they know what they want on crime and justice. (2–3)

Many of the recommendations made in the Casey Review were subsequently included in the government's Green Paper *Engaging Communities in Criminal Justice*. These included the adoption of a 'single confidence measure' to monitor public assessments of the partnership work between the police and local authorities, the branding of unpaid work carried out by offenders as part of their sentence as 'Community Payback', the use of orange bibs for offenders undertaking such work, the recruitment and training of a body of volunteer 'Community Crimefighters', and an increasing emphasis on publicising crime data and sentencing outcomes at the local level.

2.5 Conclusion

During the 1970s and 1980s researchers expressed reservations about the value of 'general' measures of public opinion which they saw as generating misleading findings due to poor levels of public knowledge about the 'reality' of crime and criminal justice, and the inherent complexity and fluidity of public beliefs and sentiments. However, Walker and Hough (1988) made a case for general measures as providing an indicator of how the public feel about the criminal justice system overall, something which they suggested measures of opinions about what should happen in specific cases could not provide. This view was reflected in the later report by Hough and Roberts (1998), which (inadvertently) provided the blueprint for the development of research on public confidence in the criminal justice system and identified a 'crisis of confidence' in sentencing *caused by* poor levels of public knowledge about the reality of crime and criminal justice system. Their recommendation that more effort should be put into communicating with the public to provide them with an accurate appreciation of typical sentencing practice, linked to a tantalising suggestion that this 'may' help to increase confidence in the criminal justice system, proved highly influential.

The adoption of a government target to improve public confidence in the criminal justice system precipitated a rapid growth in research, and this research tended to follow the blueprint for confidence research set out by Hough and Roberts (1998). The accumulation of research into public confidence, each referencing earlier studies, and repeating similar ideas and findings, gives the impression of continuity and cumulativeness. However, the research has tended to produce repetitive findings and it is possible to point to several episodes of mis- or over-interpretation of research findings which have given the knowledge base a more solid appearance than the available evidence appears to warrant. Nonetheless, through the steady accretion of these published studies, an idea of 'public confidence in the criminal justice system' as a real, measurable thing, with identifiable causes, was constructed and linked to an agenda for policy and practice organised around educating the public about 'the facts' of crime and criminal justice.

Different approaches to achieving enhanced public knowledge were trialled through several quasi-experimental studies. In this understanding of public confidence, members of the public are understood as dependent upon 'experts' to understand the reality of crime and justice, and particular ways of knowing about crime and justice, concerned with overall aggregates, proportions, and averages are positioned as producing the most relevant forms of knowledge upon which to base opinions and assessments. Similarly, when it comes to understanding the views of the public, survey data is promoted as the most appropriate way to understand how the public think and feel. In the next chapter I unpick this way of conceptualising public confidence to identify the underlying assumptions that hold it together.

Notes

1. I included the literature on public confidence in policing as I very quickly noticed that there were no clear dividing lines in discussions of public confidence between those studies which focused on the police, and those studies focused on the criminal justice system as a whole. The research on those topics used similar methods and approaches, suggesting that both were shaped by similar rationalities.
2. I developed this shorthand way to describe this approach to public opinion in two earlier publications (Turner 2014, 2016).
3. A review of the UK literature on 'public confidence in the criminal justice system' found that purely quantitative studies dramatically outnumbered qualitative studies (Turner et al. 2007).
4. The Royal Commission was appointed by the Prime Minister in April 1964. Its terms of reference stated that its purpose was 'in the light of modern knowledge of crime, and its causes, and of modern penal practice here and abroad, to re-examine the concepts and purposes which should underlie the punishment and treatment of offenders in England and Wales; to report how far they are realised by the penalties and methods of treatment available to the courts, and whether any changes in these, or in the arrangements and responsibility for selecting the sentences to be imposed on particular offend-

ers, are desirable; to review the work of the services and institutions dealing with offenders, and the responsibility for their administration: and to make recommendations'. No report was produced and the Royal Commission was decommissioned in May 1966 upon the appointment by the Home Secretary of a standing Advisory Council on the Penal System.

5. In many ways the public confidence issue closely parallels the debates around how to measure and address fear of crime. Traditionally, administrative criminologists and some CJS practitioners saw the 'problem' of fear of crime as a situation where lay people failed to rationalistically process the available data on their probability of becoming a victim (Lupton and Tulloch 1999: 508). The media were held responsible by many criminal justice professionals and commentators for, amongst other things, increasing the fear of crime, distorting people's perceptions of the prevalence of all types of crime, but particularly of violent and sexual crime, and damaging public understandings of sentencing by focusing disproportionately on atypical cases (Pratt 2007; Roberts et al. 2003; Hough 2003; Allen 2004). There was thus a tendency to see the public expression of an inappropriate level of fear (or confidence) as a 'dysfunction' of the public (Lupton and Tulloch 1999: 508) stemming from their propensity to hold inaccurate beliefs about the incidence of crime.
6. At the national level, in 2003 two different pieces of research were commissioned by the Home Office from commercial research organisations. Research carried out by MORI (Page et al. 2004) was published as part of the Home Office's 'Findings' series of papers and subsequently cited in two Ministry of Justice studies (Smith 2007; Singer and Cooper 2008). NOP World in partnership with Phillip Gould Associates (PGA) were commissioned to carry out qualitative research to 'uncover what drives confidence in the CJS as a whole, and in its separate agencies and to help the Home Office develop strategies to harness these drivers' (NOP World 2003). The research has not been externally published by the Home Office; however, it has subsequently been cited in one of their own research reports (Rix et al. 2009), suggesting that it had some internal influence. In addition to these nationally commissioned studies, several studies were carried out at the local level, usually by or on behalf of Local Criminal Justice Boards seeking support for their efforts to meet the centrally imposed confidence targets. The influence of local research on the dominant knowledge discourse of confidence appears to have been limited as most of it was reported locally, but not subsequently cited elsewhere. However, this research has tended to replicate the approaches used in the national-level research, rediscovering on a 'local' basis knowledge about confidence that is already in circulation. See Appendix 1 for further detail on some of these studies. For a more detailed discussion, see Turner (2008).

7. Hammersley (1995) has noted that the dominant model for Western governments' social research, the 'Engineering Model', sees the end product of research as modifying policy and society. He argues that this means that '[t] he parameters of the inquiry process are set narrowly: the aim is to solve the problem, and both the problem and what constitutes a solution are defined by practitioners' (126).
8. See Appendix 1 for more information.
9. This was something that, as a researcher working within a criminal justice organisation, I experienced at meetings and in conversations with colleagues. I also attended conferences of practitioners where personnel from MORI presented their findings.

References

Allen, R. 2004. What Works in Changing Public Attitudes: Lessons from Rethinking Crime and Punishment. *Journal for Crime, Conflict and the Media* 1 (3): 55–67.

Allen, J., M. El Komy, J. Lovbakke, and H. Roy. 2005. *Policing and the Criminal Justice System – Public Confidence and Perceptions: Findings from the 2003/04 British Crime Survey*. London: Home Office.

Banks, C., E. Maloney, and H. Willcock. 1975. Public Attitudes to Crime and the Penal System. *British Journal of Criminology* 15 (3): 228–240.

Bottoms, Anthony. 1995. The Philosophy and Politics of Punishment and Sentencing. In *The Politics of Sentencing Reform*, ed. Chris Clarkson and Rod Morgan, 17–49. Oxford: Clarendon.

Casey, L. 2008. *Engaging Communities in Fighting Crime*. London: Cabinet Office.

Chapman, Becca, Catriona Mirrlees-Black, and Claire Brawn. 2002. *Improving Public Attitudes to the Criminal Justice System: The Impact of Information*. London: Home Office.

Doob, Anthony N., and Julian V. Roberts. 1984. Social Psychology, Social Attitudes, and Attitudes Towards Sentencing. *Canadian Journal of Behavioural Science* 16 (4): 269–280.

———. 1988. Public Punitiveness and Public Knowledge of the Facts: Some Canadian Surveys. In *Public Attitudes to Sentencing: Surveys from Five Countries*, ed. N. Walker and M. Hough, 111–133. Aldershot: Gower.

Duffy, B., R. Wake, T. Burrows, and P. Bremner. 2007. *Closing the Gaps: Crime and Public Perceptions*. London: Ipsos MORI.

Flanagan, Sir Ronnie. 2008. *The Review of Policing: Final Report*. London: Home Office.

Hammersley, M. 1995. *The Politics of Social Research*. London: Sage.

Hough, Mike. 2003. Modernization and Public Opinion: Some Criminal Justice Paradoxes. *Contemporary Politics* 9 (2): 143–155.
Hough, Mike, and Patricia Mayhew. 1983. *The British Crime Survey: First Report.* London: Her Majesty's Stationary Office.
———. 1985. *Taking Account of Crime: Key Findings From the Second British Crime Survey.* London: Home Office.
Hough, Mike, and David Moxon. 1985. Dealing with Offenders: Popular Opinion and the Views of Victims – Findings from the British Crime Survey. *The Howard Journal* 24 (3): 160–175.
Hough, Mike, and Julian V. Roberts. 1998. *Attitudes to Punishment: Findings from the British Crime Survey.* London: Home Office.
Lupton, D., and J. Tulloch. 1999. Theorizing Fear of Crime: Beyond the Rational/ Irrational Opposition. *British Journal of Sociology* 50 (3): 507–523.
Matthews, R. 2009. Beyond 'So What?' Criminology: Rediscovering Realism. *Theoretical Criminology* 13 (3): 341–362.
Mattinson, Joanna, and Catriona Mirrlees-Black. 2000. *Attitudes to Crime and Criminal Justice: Findings from the 1998 British Crime Survey.* London: Home Office.
Mirrlees-Black, Catriona. 2001. *Confidence in the Criminal Justice System: Findings from the 2000 British Crime Survey.* London: Home Office.
NOP World. 2003. *Drivers of Confidence in the Criminal Justice System.* London: Home Office.
O'Farrell, Clare. 2005. *Michel Foucault.* London: Sage.
Page, B., R. Wake, and A. Ames. 2004. *Home Office Findings 221: Public Confidence in the Criminal Justice System.* London: Home Office.
Pratt, John. 2007. *Penal Populism.* Abingdon: Routledge.
Rix, A., F. Joshua, M. Maguire, and S. Morton. 2009. *Home Office Research Report 28: Improving Public Confidence in the Police: A Review of the Evidence.* London: Home Office.
Robert, Philippe. 1978. *The Extent of Public Information and the Nature of Public Attitudes Towards the Social Control of Crime.* Council of Europe 13th Criminological Research Conference: Public Opinion on Crime and Criminal Justice.
Roberts, Julian V., and Anthony N. Doob. 1989. Sentencing and Public Opinion: Taking False Shadows for True Substances. *Osgoode Hall Law Journal* 27 (3): 491–503.
Roberts, Julian V., and Mike Hough, eds. 2002. *Changing Attitudes to Punishment: Public Opinion, Crime and Justice.* Cullompton: Willan.
———. 2005a. Sentencing Young Offenders: Public Opinion in England and Wales. *Criminal Justice* 5 (3): 211–232.
———. 2005b. The State of the Prisons: Exploring Public Knowledge and Opinion. *The Howard Journal* 44 (3): 286–306.

———. 2005c. *Understanding Public Attitudes to Criminal Justice*. Maidenhead: Open University Press.
Roberts, Julian V., Loretta J. Stalans, David Indermaur, and Mike Hough. 2003. *Penal Populism and Public Opinion: Lessons from Five Countries*. Oxford: Oxford University Press.
Rock, Paul. 1979. *Public Opinion and Criminal Legislation*. Council of Europe 13th Criminological Research Conference: Public Opinion on Crime and Criminal Justice.
Salisbury, Heather. 2004. *Public Attitudes to the Criminal Justice System: The Impact of Providing Information to British Crime Survey Respondents*. London: Home Office.
Schneider, Hans Joachim. 1978. *The Influence of Mass Communication Media on Public Opinion on Crime and Criminal Justice*. Council of Europe 13th Criminological Research Conference: Public Opinion on Crime and Criminal Justice.
Shaw, Stephen. 1982. *The People's Justice: A Major Poll of Public Attitudes on Crime and Punishment*. London: Prison Reform Trust.
Singer, Lawrence, and Suzanne Cooper. 2008. *Inform, Persuade and Remind: An Evaluation of a Project to Improve Public Confidence in the Criminal Justice System*. London: Ministry of Justice.
Smith, D. 2007. *Confidence in the Criminal Justice System: What Lies Beneath?* London: Ministry of Justice.
Turner, L., E. Campbell, A. Dale, and R. Graham. 2007. *Creating a Knowledge-Base of Public Confidence in the Criminal Justice System—Report 2: Literature Review*. Newcastle Upon Tyne: Newcastle University.
Turner, Liz. 2008. Public Confidence in the Criminal Justice System: The Impact of a Dominant National-Level Discourse on Research and Practice. *Crime Prevention and Community Safety: An International Journal* 10 (3): 174–189.
———. 2014. Penal Populism, Deliberative Methods and the Production of 'Public Opinion' on Crime and Punishment. *The Good Society* 23 (1): 87–102.
Turner, Elizabeth R. 2016. Mass Incarceration and Public Opinion on Crime and Justice: From Democratic Theory to Method and Reality. In *Democratic Theory and Mass Incarceration*, ed. Albert W. Dzur, Ian Loader, and Richard Sparks, 213–237. Oxford: Oxford University Press.
Van Dijk, J.M. 1979. *The Extent of Public Information and the Nature of Public Attitudes Towards Crime*. Council of Europe Thirteenth Criminological Research Conference: Public Opinion on Crime and Criminal Justice.
Walker, Nigel, and Mike Hough, eds. 1988. *Public Attitudes to Sentencing: Surveys from Five Countries*. Aldershot: Gower.
Whitehead, E., and J. Taylor. 2003. Public Confidence in the Criminal Justice System. In *Crime in England and Wales 2001/02: Supplementary Volume*, ed. C. Taylor and J. Flood-Page, 119–134. London: Home Office.

CHAPTER 3

Deconstructing Public Confidence: The Public Confidence Agenda as a Governmental Project

Abstract In order to produce knowledge about confidence, researchers use 'procedures of intervention' that come between the things to be known and representations of those things: this constitutes a 'violation'. *All* knowledge, whether derived from a survey or a deliberative process, involves researchers choosing procedures that violate what they study. The decisions they make, then, are about *how* to violate reality in order to arrive at knowledge. The dominant approach to public confidence research constructs a hierarchy of objects: reality, representations, perceptions, feelings. The solution to the confidence problem is understood as that of correcting perceptions through better representations of reality. This dominant conceptualisation of public confidence privileges expert ways of knowing. Deliberative approaches, promoting dialogue, are unfairly dismissed as unable to access the 'reality' of public opinion. But this view fails to acknowledge that all ways of knowing about public opinion must produce the phenomenon they go on to represent.

Keywords Foucault • Governmentality • Public confidence in criminal justice • Media distortion of crime • Public understanding of criminal justice • Public knowledge • Deliberative methods

E.R. Turner, *Public Confidence in Criminal Justice*,
Critical Criminological Perspectives,
https://doi.org/10.1007/978-3-319-67897-9_3

This chapter starts from the position that the quest to improve public confidence in the criminal justice system, and the whole gamut of investigations, recommendations, strategies, and tactics that sprang up to serve this cause collectively constitute what Foucault termed a 'regime of practices': 'programmes of conduct which have both prescriptive effects regarding what is to be done (effects of "jurisdiction"), and codifying effects regarding what is to be known (effects of "veridiction")' (Foucault 1991, 75). In Foucauldian thought, regimes of practices are not understood as more or less 'rational', rather 'forms of rationality' are inscribed within 'practices or systems of practices' as '"practices" don't exist without a certain regime of rationality' (79). The analysis of regimes of practices, then, seeks to identify two things: (1) the ensemble of rules and procedures which they contain and (2) how they set up a 'domain of objects about which it is possible to articulate true or false propositions' (79).

In this chapter, I analyse the literature on public confidence as part of a 'regime of practices', identifying how statements in the dominant discourse of public confidence are predicated upon the existence of several related objects envisaged by the researchers as existing in specific positions in relation to one another (placed in a 'grid of specification' in Foucauldian terminology). I provide examples of the common 'procedures of intervention' used to produce knowledge on public confidence, and argue that these procedures should be seen as only one way in which knowledge might be produced: other ways of knowing are possible. However, as I also show, the tendency in the literature has been to deny or conceal this possibility by suggesting that the dominant survey-based approach to confidence is the only way to capture and represent the reality of public confidence, and that other methods, whilst capable of providing useful contextual information about confidence, confront respondents with artificial dilemmas and thus provide knowledge about 'unreal' phenomena. I contest this position, arguing that it obscures the researchers' inevitable political entanglements, and in so doing evades the ethical responsibilities that ought to be considered as researchers leave ontological ripples in their wake.

3.1 Identifying Objects in the 'Grid of Specification'

Mapping the grid of specification within a discourse enables us to probe 'the systematic ways that phenomena are rendered accessible to us' (Kendall and Whickham 1999, 28), including any hierarchical relationships implied between the objects which the grid contains. But identifying objects and their inter-relations is not simply a matter of apprehending the meanings attached to the different words used to make statements and the way these words are explicitly placed in relation to one another. A broad conceptual vocabulary has been used to capture and describe a range of subjectivities with respect to crime and the criminal justice system. Reference is made to the following: thoughts, beliefs, and feelings; responses, moods, and sentiments; consciousness, perceptions, and views; concerns, complaints, and attitudes; opinions, preferences, and priorities; desires, wants, and demands, to name just a selection.

Ambiguities and discrepancies in the way words are deployed indicate that maintaining clear conceptual boundaries between objects is extremely difficult in everyday speech and writing about the subjective. In many cases variation in the vocabulary used appears to be a stylistic habit, but in some reports the distinction made between the different words used to denote subjectivities is treated as being of explanatory importance, for example Doob and Roberts (1984, 270) state that they

> will be using the word belief to refer to people's understanding of their environment – in this case, their criminal justice system. A belief about the criminal justice system, then, might refer to a view of what kinds of things were happening in the courts. These might form the basis of an attitude about the activities of the court: whether, for example, the sentences are appropriate.

However, even within such reports and articles, there can be slippage, as words which have at one point been given a specific conceptual meaning (such as 'belief' above) are subsequently deployed in a quite different sense within the same piece of writing. Care needs to be taken, then, when identifying the objects within public confidence discourse. We should not confuse the objects with the vocabulary used to describe them.

The imprecise and unreliable nature of the words used to describe the content of the subjective is demonstrated in public confidence discourse in the interchangeable usage of certain words, for example 'think' and 'believe'. Both words are used to make statements about facts and more normative concerns. For example, Roberts and Doob (1989, 494) observed a 'very real discrepancy between what people think sentences to be and what, in fact, they are'. The authors use 'think' here to indicate factual belief. However, in an earlier piece (Doob and Roberts 1988), they stated that 'policy makers, politicians, and others who wish to listen carefully to what members of the Canadian public really know and think about the sentencing of criminal offenders will find that the public's view of sentencing is not simple and shallow' (132). Here to 'think' is contrasted with to 'know', suggesting that the thinking is normative or evaluative, rather than being a factual belief. Ten years later, one of the same authors, now working in a different partnership (Hough and Roberts 1998) makes this same distinction between knowing and thinking, setting up the contrast between 'knowledge and opinion' and referring to what people 'know and think about sentencing' (1).

The use of the word 'belief' to refer to factual judgements, can be seen, for example, when Hough and Mayhew (1985, 43) refer to 'the accuracy of public beliefs about current sentencing practice' and Roberts and Hough (1998, 34) observe that 'the British public do want harsher sentences (or at least harsher than they believe them to be).' However, in other statements the belief referred to is at once factual and normative; for example 'a substantial portion of Canadians believe that sentences are not severe enough' (Doob and Roberts 1988, 111) and 'less than 10 per cent of a national sample believed that the police were too tough' (Hindelang 1974, 106). The same lack of clarity also appears in statements using the word 'think'; for example 'even with criminals more likely to get jail sentences than 10 years ago, average sentence lengths longer and prisoner numbers at an all-time high, the public think sentencing is still too lenient' (Casey 2008, 5). A further concept used as a synonym for thinking/believing is the notion of having a 'view'. Like thoughts and beliefs, views can be factual, as in, 'attempt to convey a more accurate view of sentencing to the public' (Roberts and Doob 1989, 496), and more normative, as in, 'the negative view of sentencing attributed to the public' (Roberts and Doob 1989, 498).

Use of the word 'feel' is perhaps even more ambiguous as, in addition to indicating factual or normative beliefs, the notion of feeling can also be used to flag up a physical sensation or emotional reaction to something. When used to indicate a factual belief, the 'feeling' in question is a feeling that the facts are X, for example 'respondents were asked whether they felt that "our system of law enforcement works to really discourage people from committing crime"' (Hindelang 1974, 105). As with the words think and believe, some statements using the word 'feel' were apparently factual and normative at the same time, whilst other statements more clearly separated views of the facts from normative feelings; for example 'those who underestimated the severity of the courts [FACTUAL BELIEF] tended in general to feel that court sentences were not tough enough [NORMATIVE BELIEF]' (Hough et al. 1988, 208); 'the public views crime as being more violent than it seems to be [FACTUAL]; sees the justice system as responding too leniently [FACTUAL AND NORMATIVE], and in some instances more leniently than it in fact does; and feels changes should be made in this system[NORMATIVE]' (Doob and Roberts 1984, 272). Further statements refer to how people 'feel' about or because of what they know, for example '[t]he public feel let down' (Casey 2008, 46).

The examples given above indicate that within the confidence discourse (and its antecedents in more general attitudinal research) there are no stable objects which can be inferred purely from the use of words like 'think', 'believe', 'view', or 'feel'. Yet, although the conceptual vocabulary is often imprecise, throughout the confidence discourse a clear (albeit mostly implicit) distinction is made between what people think/believe/feel/view/perceive/see to be 'the facts' of reality and what they think/believe/feel about or because of their understanding of those facts. This distinction is well illustrated in the following statement from Hough and Roberts (1998): '[t]he public are dissatisfied with sentencing practice, *or what they perceive sentencing practice to be*' (Hough and Roberts 1998, 2, *emphasis added*). This statement makes clear distinctions between three categories of object: (1) the reality of crime and criminal justice ('sentencing practice'), (2) public factual beliefs about reality ('what they perceive sentencing practice to be'), and (3) public feelings towards reality ('dissatisfied'). Implicit in this statement (and indeed in many of the other statements included above) is that public perceptions of reality often differ from the actual 'facts' of reality.

The media are frequently identified as the source of public ignorance about crime and the criminal justice system, said to provide 'incomplete reports' (Walker and Hough 1988, 10); and 'a distorted picture of sentencing policy and practice' (Roberts and Doob 1989, 499) in stories which are 'brief and provide the reader with little information about the case or the relevant sentencing provisions' (Roberts and Doob 1989, 500) and which fail to place individual crimes in the context of general crime statistics (see Pratt 2007; Roberts et al. 2003; Roberts and Hough 2002; Allen 2002). Descriptions of the tone and content of media reporting objectify these representations, and contrast them to other representations, for example 'statistics about falling crime' (Hough and Roberts 1998, 8), 'data on the actual crime situation' (Van Dijk 1979, 39), and 'a balanced picture of crime' (Hough and Mayhew 1983, 35). The types of representations which are deemed to be appropriate if the public are to be 'properly' informed tend to be statistical and/or aggregating or averaging, for example the proportion of crime that is violent, the 'typical' sentences received for certain crimes, or the proportion of offenders sentenced to prison for specific offences. To the three objects identified above (the *reality* of crime and criminal justice, public factual beliefs about (or *perceptions* of) reality, and public *feelings* towards reality) we can now add *representations* of the facts of reality. The literature implies that such representations often come between the actual facts and public beliefs about those facts.

A key characteristic of the dominant discourse of public confidence, then, is that it implicitly delineates and relies upon four categories of 'object' which are clearly linked in a causal schema. Representations of reality are regarded as more or less satisfactory attempts to reflect reality. Public beliefs about reality are seen as conditioned and informed by public exposure to different representations of reality (and sometimes also by unmediated exposure to reality). Public feelings about the criminal justice system are assumed to be prompted by their beliefs about the reality of that system. Thus, the 'grid of specification' which operates in relation to the 'objects' which feature in public confidence discourse is essentially hierarchical, with the (implicitly monolithic and accessible) reality of crime and criminal justice at the apex. What concerns the researchers and policy-makers who make confidence their business is the lack of alignment between reality and beliefs about reality, which, they suggest, can be caused by faulty representations of reality and lead to negative feelings about reality.

3.2 Violating the 'Things to Be Known'

To construct the 'grid of specification' described above, researchers impose categories and causal schema on the stuff of reality. The Foucauldian notion of 'procedures of intervention' describes the regulation of processes for introducing new statements into a discursive field. This takes place when statements are transposed from one discursive context into another (Hughes and Sharrock 2007, 331), for example from an individual respondent making an on-the-spot selection of a response option in a survey, into the conclusions of a report produced based on the aggregation of multiple such moments. Drawing on Nietzsche, Foucault arrived at the view that

> knowledge must struggle against a world without order, without connectedness, without form, without beauty, without wisdom, without harmony, and without law ... Knowledge can only be a violation of the things to be known, and not a perception, a recognition, an identification of or with those things. (Foucault 1994, 9)

When categorising reality to represent it, researchers follow the rules and conventions of method which regulate the statements which they may introduce into the 'discursive field' of social research. But, however faithful the researcher to the rules laid down by their discipline, their categories and frameworks must still *intervene* between the 'things to be known' and possible understandings of those things, resulting in a 'violation'.

Within the public confidence discourse two 'procedures of intervention' are routinely used. Firstly, most reports on findings from research on confidence produce statements about what people *really* think/feel/believe based on the option they select in response to a closed question from an interviewer, or on a questionnaire. Secondly, within such research, where a statistical association exists between the selection of one response option and the selection of another or others, it is conventional to report this as indicating a *real* link between *real* phenomena, something which is often taken to indicate a degree of causality from one variable to another.

Such procedures of intervention can be seen at work in the following paragraph:

> Averaging the estimates of imprisonment rates for the three crimes shows the contrast between respondents who believe sentences are much too lenient and the rest of the sample. Averaged across the offences, respondents who felt sentences are much too lenient believed that 38 per cent of offenders were incarcerated. The average for those who felt sentences were a little too lenient was 42 per cent, and those who thought sentences were about right or too tough generated an average of 47 per cent. This suggests that ignorance about current practice is one source of public dissatisfaction with sentencing. (Hough and Roberts 1998, 21)

Within this paragraph it is possible to discern a number of 'violations' of the 'things to be known': (1) knowledge about the 'current practice' of the criminal justice system is taken to be adequately represented by 'estimates of imprisonment rates'; (2) 'public dissatisfaction with sentencing' is understood as indicated by those having selected the option 'much too lenient' or 'a little too lenient' (significantly, those who selected the option of saying that sentences are 'too tough' have their selection lumped in with those who selected the option 'about right'; the selection of the option 'too tough' indicates dissatisfaction in a direction which is commonly rendered invisible); (3) the increase in the average estimates of the percentage of offenders jailed, which is observed as respondents become more satisfied, is taken to indicate that 'ignorance about current practice' is a '*source* of public dissatisfaction with sentencing' (*emphasis added*).

A similar order of 'violation' can also be observed in the following statement: 'instrumental worries about personal safety were not, in fact, the driver of public confidence in policing. Feeling that one's local community lacked cohesion, social trust and informal social control was much more important' (Jackson and Sunshine 2007, 18). As with the excerpt from Hough and Roberts (1998) above, this statement is made based on an analysis of the statistical associations between variables. In the statement, Jackson and Sunshine do not distinguish between their operationalisation of the concepts which they are studying (confidence, worries, feelings) and the phenomena (or 'things') themselves. As such they imply an identity between the measures applied and the phenomena studied, encouraging the reader to understand the phenomena called into being by their questionnaire as manifestations of 'real' things, or 'social facts'. In both this and the previous example, the data used provide us with no way of knowing how the relationships inferred from the observed statistical associations would be reflected in what the respondents would have said if asked to explain *in their own words* why they may or may not be confident.

To make this rather obvious point about the inherent limitations of quantitative data is *not* to say that the researchers are not making valid observations according to 'procedures of intervention' accepted as conventional within their field (although confusing statistical association with causality is generally frowned upon). Rather it is to flag up the not-insignificant point that these statements, and the analytical techniques upon which they are premised, are 'procedures of intervention' which serve to *transform* the observed behaviour of individual members of the public within the research environment into something which is both other than what it actually was (the expression of an on the spot estimation, the choice of a pre-defined response option), and also other than what it might be if the same topics were addressed under different conditions.

Qualitative studies, which might provide a rather different way of understanding public confidence, have proved much less influential than quantitative studies in shaping the dominant discourse of public confidence. The dominance of quantitative methods in the public confidence research agenda may be due to policymakers favouring 'hard' numerical data over the 'rich' data which is usually generated by semi-structured interviews and focus groups. But, arguably, researchers themselves should assume some responsibility for determining which methods of research are regarded as acceptable within the public confidence agenda, and which have thus contributed to the dominant discourse of public confidence. Where qualitative studies of public confidence have been carried out they have tended to explore what respondents understand by terms such as 'public confidence' and 'criminal justice system', and what they think about when deciding how to answer closed survey questions. For example, in a report for the Ministry of Justice carried out several years after the introduction of the general confidence target, Smith (2007, 14) seeks to find out, 'What factors do people think about when deciding how confident they are in the CJS?' Such research is positioned in an auxiliary role as compared to quantitative studies, at times functioning like a form of retrospective cognitive testing but, rather than findings being used to refine the indicators so that they capture what is intended,[1] they are used to try and 'increase' positive performance against these indicators.

The public confidence research agenda also creates conditions for a third procedure of intervention which occurs when survey responses come to be understood as 'demands' or 'wants'. In this way responses which are deliberately elicited by researchers through a survey are conflated with members of the public proactively saying something or making demands. For example, Duffy et al. (2007, 16) refer to the government's willingness to address 'the priorities that come up consistently in research studies' as 'giving people what they say they want'. In this way research studies like those described above may also be treated as expressions of what the public 'really' demand or want from their government, indicating their considerable political potential.

3.3 'Reality Effects'

That research can have political consequences is hardly a startling, or unwelcome, suggestion. But it is worth considering the different ways in which such consequences come to pass. For it is not merely the final product of research—knowledge—that can influence wider society and political actors. Rather, the way research is conducted implies some underlying assumptions about the nature of social reality, political citizenship, and the possibilities of knowledge production. These assumptions can themselves have effects.

Recent years have seen many effective critiques of the adequacy of quantitative survey data as applied to the matter of public opinion (e.g. see Fishkin 1995; Ackerman and Fishkin 2004; Price and Neijens 1997; Shamir and Shamir 2000). It has been frequently suggested that mass survey data tends 'to collect and disseminate opinions that may be ill-informed "non-attitudes" or "pseudo-opinions" developed outside of any meaningful public debate' (Price and Neijens 1997, 337). The mass survey is seen as having undermined and usurped an earlier understanding of public opinion as a phenomenon formed and expressed in the context of social interaction, sidelining the more active, engaged, deliberative notion of a public that prevailed during the eighteenth, nineteenth, and early twentieth centuries (see Bellah et al. 2008; Mills 2000). Arguably, what aggregating surveys capture is not *public* opinion at all. Rather, in failing to open a conversation with their participants, they produce summaries of '*private* opinions' (Bellah et al. 2008, 305).

Despite criticisms of this kind, the opinion survey has been a ubiquitous feature of the political landscape for decades. The longer it is with us, the harder it seems to be to dislodge. In the age of the opinion survey individuals are repeatedly exposed to claims about public opinion based on survey data, increasing the risk that surveys are having 'deeper cognitive effects on how people remember, envision, and think about public opinion and the public that has opinions' (Beniger 1992, 217). Bourdieu (1984) argued that this led to the emergence of an 'opinionated habitus': a set of sociopolitical dispositions moulded by and to dominant ways of knowing about public opinion. Similarly, Osborne and Rose (1999, 392) propose that 'people *learn* to have opinions; they become "opinioned"... people come to "fit" the demands of the research; they become, so to speak, persons that are by nature "researchable" from that perspective.' This learned subject position sees people thinking and behaving as if they hold, and are entitled to hold, their own individual opinions on a whole range of issues, prior to and independently of the moment they are asked to produce such an opinion by a researcher, and irrespective of their previous knowledge of the issue they have been asked about, and the opinions of others who may be more knowledgeable about or affected by the issue in question. In calling into being political citizens of this kind, the opinion survey produces 'reality effects' (382).

As a result, the dominant approach to public opinion has implications for the way that individual citizens think about themselves as political actors. Given the political salience of research on public opinion, it would be difficult to dispute that such research can have 'costs' for the way we live together (as will be discussed further in the concluding chapter, Chapter Six). Opinion research is rarely (if ever) only research. It can, and frequently does, transmit (or attempt to transmit) information to politicians about public preferences[2]. As such, opinion research is always both an intellectual endeavour and a political practice. As Saward (2003, 166) observes:

> Democratic principles come alive (are "lived") through the medium of formal decisional mechanisms or devices which are designed to activate them and come to be justified in terms of them.

Rather than merely providing a 'workable empirical rendering' (Price and Neijens 1997, 336) of reality, then, researchers of public opinion are engaged in *enacting* a version of reality (cf. Law 2004): their surveys are devices which activate democratic principles.

Where survey research is promoted as the most legitimate channel for public expressions of confidence, or a lack thereof, this may effectively divert attention from, if not devalue, alternative channels through which the public may express their views. Indeed, Drury (2002 41) has written of how 'collectives, and crowds in particular, have historically been much maligned. A wealth of linguistic and conceptual resources has developed which has served to discredit and delegitimize the crowd.'

Crowds, including participants in mass protests, are routinely dismissed or pathologised, for failing to utilise existing legitimate (and less socially disruptive or inconvenient) mechanisms to communicate their views. But it is not merely that the confidence research agenda can devalue non-research channels through which the public may give expression to their views. It is also that, in its dominant form, it has actively suppressed or rejected alternative research-based ways of understanding how the public think and feel about crime and the criminal justice system. Several studies carried out over the last 20 years suggest potentially fruitful alternative methods for engaging with the public to explore their views about crime and justice. However, these have remained very much at the periphery of the public confidence research agenda, apparently crowded out, neutralised, or actively rejected by those engaged in more conventional survey-based research.

3.4 The Real and the Unreal: Relocating the Problem

As noted in the previous chapter, some researchers initially cautioned against reliance on general opinion measures (which failed to consider the extent of public ignorance about actual sentencing trends) and argued in favour of 'more sophisticated survey questions' (Roberts and Doob 1989, 514), which elicited respondents' preferences in relation to particular sentencing scenarios. They proposed this as a way to access the 'true substances' of public opinion, rather than the 'false shadows' generated by measures of the general opinion of a public considered to be largely ignorant of important facts about the workings of justice.

However, Walker and Hough (1988) offered a different perspective. They argued that, despite their shortcomings, general measures of opinion had value as a measure of 'generalized satisfaction' because such opinions exist in 'real life', whereas opinion on appropriate practice in specific cases must be deliberately constructed through the research mechanism.

> If a survey is intended to gauge public confidence in sentencing, there is a case for limiting details to the sort of information which ordinary members of the public get from newspapers, radio or television. To give respondents anymore is to put them in a position in which they will not find themselves in real life, where they form their opinions on sentencing. (220)

They defend the retention of general opinion questions, despite them having been described elsewhere as 'insufficiently precise', 'false shadows', and 'useless for policy'.

Hough and Roberts (1998) developed this line of argument further, referring back to what they referred to as the 'experiment' carried out by Roberts and Doob (1989) and suggesting that it showed that 'information … is critical to public attitudes to sentencing. As a general rule, the less information that people have about any specific case, the more likely they are to advocate a punitive response to it … the amount of information about a case is critical in determining public reaction' (Hough and Roberts 1998, 2–3). However, by referring to the approach to gauging attitudes taken by Roberts and Doob (1989) as an 'experiment', Hough and Roberts positioned it as creating 'unreal' conditions, echoing Walker and Hough's assertion that giving respondents more information than they would receive through the newspapers 'is to put them in a position in which they will not find themselves in real life' (see above).

In these, and other reports making similar claims, the reader is presented with two distinctive phenomena: a general sense of cynicism or confidence in sentencing which *pre-exists* research, and sentencing preferences which, it is implied, are only activated by the more complex and specific types of survey questions which provide respondents with additional information. So, despite recognising that these two phenomena are simply different (rather than 'true' or 'false' representations of a pre-existing reality), both Walker and Hough (1988) and then Hough and Roberts (1998) place them in an implicit hierarchy. The more hypothetical forms of opinion elicited through more complex and specific survey questions are portrayed as interesting, and valid, but also unreal: they exist *only* because they have been drawn out of the public in the survey context.

An alternative way of looking at this issue is this: the responses obtained through the different questioning approaches are both *equally artificial*, both having been brought into existence by the different questioning techniques. From this perspective, to assign these phenomena the labels of 'true' and 'false' or to suggest that they are real and unreal works to obscure the fact that *the researcher constructs both types of opinion*. Correspondingly, the choice between the two is not one of methodological adequacy but of ontological politics (see Law 2004): it is not what does exist and how it can be measured that is at stake, but what can be brought into existence and, crucially whether it *should* be.

However, advocates of the aggregative, general, atomised, passive (AGAP) approach to public confidence have tended to deny, evade, or conceal the possibility that the researcher has any such choice. What is essentially a political value-judgement about how best to approach a complicated and deeply political area of research is misrepresented as a more prosaic matter of determining which method best gets at a reality that is assumed to be stable and singular and to pre-exist the researchers' 'interventions'. Rather than being a reason to change the research method used to understand public opinion, the problem of poor public knowledge is repositioned within the 'grid of specification' (see above) as a causal factor. This deftly relocates the problem from the realm of subjective, value-judgements about how best to produce knowledge in a particular area, to that of objectively determining the most appropriate scientific mechanism to capture reality. This relocation facilitates the denial and concealment of the idea that things could be other, aiding proponents of the survey-based AGAP approach in minimising the potential of developing more deliberative approaches to public opinion.

3.5 Undermining Alternative Approaches: Dismissing Deliberation

The advantages of deliberative approaches in relation to crime and criminal justice have been noted by, among others, Green (2006, 2008), Loader (2011), and Loader and Sparks (2011). Green (2006, 131) argues that attempts to educate the public about the facts of crime and criminal justice are of limited utility due to their failure to have an enduring impact on public preferences and opinions. Loader (2011, 349) describes the educational approach as the 'cognitive deficit model' and suggests that it signally fails to address the intense emotions which issues of crime and punishment can provoke. As a solution, he proposes the 'redirection model', which would seek to

> fashion institutions and institutional practices that mediate between public sensibilities and crime control policy ... bringing the emotionally laced experience and demands of citizens in from the shadows ... opening them up to the scrutiny of public, communicative reason. (356)

Green (2006) provides a more detailed account of one method which might be used to achieve Loader's vision for redirection. He explores the background to 'deliberative polling', how it would work and what its benefits would be, contrasting the 'shallow, unconsidered public *opinion*' captured through polls and surveys, with the 'reflective, informed public judgment' which a deliberative poll can produce (132). The purpose, he argues, is to 'help produce an informed, more defensibly invoked public will' (133).

Advocates of the greater use of deliberative methods argue that traditional survey-based methods capture 'shallow, unconsidered' responses (Green 2006, 132) or what Fishkin (2009) has called 'raw' and 'debilitated' opinion, and should be replaced (or at least supplemented) with mechanisms which require participants to engage with 'facts' and participate in deliberation with fellow citizens (see, e.g. Dzur 2012; Dzur and Mirchandani 2007; Fishkin 1995; Green 2006, 2008; Loader 2011; Loader and Sparks 2010; Luskin et al. 2002). The overarching purpose of deploying a deliberative approach is to support participants in going beyond 'mere opinion' (Dzur and Mirchandani 2007, 168) and towards more 'refined' opinions (Fishkin 2009). Deliberative methods attempt to reconfigure the phenomenon we have come to know as 'public opinion' to provide more 'defensible' (Green 2008, 242) assessments of what members of the public expect from the criminal justice system.

In 2002, along with Alison Park form the National Centre for Social Research (NatCen), Mike Hough revisited a study from 1994 in which James Fishkin, the pioneer of 'deliberative polling' (see Fishkin 1995; 1996; Luskin et al. 2002; Ackerman and Fishkin 2004) along with NatCen and Channel 4, invited 297 people to attend a weekend-long deliberative workshop on crime and punishment. Over the course of the weekend, participants received presentations from practitioners, academics, and politicians and took part in group discussions about the issues raised (Hough and Park 2002, 167). In contrast to Green (2006, 149), who emphasises the 'democratic utility' of the deliberative poll, Hough and Park (2002, 165) seek to explore how the deliberative poll can be used to 'change public attitudes', referring to it as a 'laboratory setting for learning more about public opinion' (166).

Hough and Park represent deliberative polls as motivated by primarily 'normative', rather than 'scientific' aspirations, and as necessarily producing findings which are artificial. They contrast this with the 'real' opinions elicited through surveys. They highlight key criticisms of deliberative polls, including (unreferenced) 'critics [who] have suggested that whatever the *desirability* of having a well-informed and thoughtful public, deliberative polls are irrelevant as politicians need to take account of the reality of public opinion as it emerges from "snapshot" public opinion polls' (166). They further underline what is, in their view, the inferior status of deliberative polling in their conclusion, arguing that although 'there is an obvious need to improve on the ways that opinion on complex topics is canvassed', deliberative polls are expensive, potentially biased, and do not produce representative results which can be generalised to the wider population (181).

> Deliberative polling will never replace the standard, representative poll as a measure of public opinion. However, it may serve as a very useful adjunct and generate insight into community views that cannot be gleaned from the survey approach which carries so much weight with politicians. (182)

This conclusion implies that surveys are cheap, free from bias, and produce accurate, scientific findings about the 'reality' of public opinion. Deliberative polls on the other hand are appropriate only if used in a supporting role (as a 'useful adjunct') because they create an artificial research scenario which, however desirable, does not exist in real life. Interestingly though, Hough and Park also clearly indicate that it is the attachment of *politicians* to the consumption of survey data (rather than the inherent superiority of such data, or the attachment of some researchers to its production) that gives the survey its power.

3.6 Conclusion

In this and the previous chapter I have argued that research on public confidence in the criminal justice system developed on foundations which were laid during the 1980s, and that during the 1990s the previously prominent methodological debate about how to access 'true' public opinion on sentencing gave way to a narrower focus on how misperceptions can be addressed so that general ('real') opinion on the criminal justice system will be more favourable. The problem of inaccurate public perceptions of the crime problem and criminal justice system practice was relocated from the sphere of value-based choice-making about 'how to know' into the sphere of science: poor public knowledge became a causal factor in a model of public confidence that posited a specific, hierarchical 'grid of specification'. The objective for policymakers and practitioners was not just to ensure that actual sentencing practice was roughly 'in line' with public preferences, but also to ensure that the public would *know* that this was the case and *as a result* would hold favourable attitudes towards the criminal justice system: would say that they felt confident.

The dominant discourse of public confidence produced and maintained by the research literature constructs confidence as a real and measurable phenomenon which experts can capture, represent, and 'know' through the application of appropriate methods. Based on the findings these methods generate, it has been argued that the public frequently lack confidence in the criminal justice system because they have not adequately grasped the facts of reality. The types of 'facts' implied to be relevant include the proportions of people sentenced to imprisonment for different offence types, typical sentences for different offences, and the proportion of offences that are violent. That is to say, the kinds of objective, quantitative 'facts' that experts might consider most relevant for understanding the state of criminal justice. This dominant discourse implies an understanding of the world as one where there is a single, knowable reality of crime and criminal justice which can be represented by experts using appropriate methods.

This discourse posits an unequal relationship between experts and the lay public as expert ways of knowing about reality are privileged over lay ways of knowing. Furthermore, experts are permitted to appropriate the responses which members of the public make in an artificial context (the research context) and call them real (it is implicit in the public confidence research that such research is a legitimate way of making visible the authentic desires of the individual). One could, of course, argue that the research acts as an enabling mechanism—that it serves a useful social purpose in allowing people's demands to be heard—but, as discussed above, such a perspective ignores important criticisms of the AGAP survey approach.

The expanding body of quantitative research into the 'drivers' of public confidence, emerging since the late 1990s, has promulgated and cemented this understanding of confidence as real, measurable, and caused, and has obscured the value-judgement (about how public beliefs and feelings *should* be researched) which underpins the construction and reproduction of such a reality. Furthermore, it has cast a mould for confidence research according to which researchers already know the kinds of 'things' that they are looking for, and the 'procedures of intervention' which they should apply, and collect, code, and interpret data accordingly. The result has been that a great deal of time and resources have been spent recycling the same findings, to very little practical gain.

In the next two chapters I provide a discussion intended to shed some light on the questions posed by this dominant discourse of public confidence: (1) Why *this* 'grid of specification'? (2) Why *these* 'procedures of intervention'? (3) Why has a value-judgement been disguised? I argue that in the absence of certain 'conditions of existence' the dominant discourse of public confidence in the criminal justice system would not be 'thinkable', and that the grid of specification, procedures of intervention, and disguising of the value-judgement about how to do confidence research can be traced back to historically contingent events and ideas. I also suggest that the emergence of the public confidence agenda occurred in the context of conflict between different groups competing for power in the criminal justice and political fields, and that claims to know about public confidence should therefore also be understood as bids for power within those fields.

Notes

1. This is suggestive of the tendency identified by Williams (1998, 14) whereby 'research manages to be both operationalist and realist at the same time, asserting both the necessity of practical definition and the reality of the concepts so defined!'
2. It therefore acts as what democratic theorist John Dryzek (2000, 51) terms a 'transmission mechanism'.

References

Ackerman, Bruce, and James S. Fishkin. 2004. *Deliberation Day*. New Haven: Yale University Press.

Allen, R. 2002. "There Must Be Some Way of Dealing with Kids": Young Offenders, Public Attitudes and Policy Change. *Youth Justice* 2: 3–13.

Bellah, R.N., R. Madsen, W. Sullivan, A. Swidler, and S.M. Tipton. 2008. *Habits of the Heart: Individualism and Commitment in American Life*. Berkley: University of California Press.

Beniger, James R. 1992. The Impact of Polling on Public Opinion: Reconciling Foucault, Habermas, and Bourdieu. *International Journal of Public Opinion Research* 4 (3): 204–219.

Bourdieu, Pierre. 1984. *Distinction: A Social Critique of the Judgement of Taste*. London: Routledge.

Casey, L. 2008. *Engaging Communities in Fighting Crime*. London: Cabinet Office.

Doob, Anthony N., and Julian V. Roberts. 1984. Social Psychology, Social Attitudes, and Attitudes Towards Sentencing. *Canadian Journal of Behavioural Science* 16 (4): 269–280.

———. 1988. Public Punitiveness and Public Knowledge of the Facts: Some Canadian Surveys. In *Public Attitudes to Sentencing: Surveys from Five Countries*, ed. N. Walker and M. Hough, 111–133. Aldershot: Gower.

Drury, J. 2002. "When the Mobs are Looking for Witches to Burn, Nobody's Safe": Talking about the Reactionary Crowd. *Discourse and Society* 13 (1): 41–73.

Dryzek, John S. 2000. *Deliberative Democracy and Beyond: Liberals, Critics, Contestations*. Oxford: Oxford University Press.

Duffy, B., R. Wake, T. Burrows, and P. Bremner. 2007. *Closing the Gaps: Crime and Public Perceptions*. London: Ipsos MORI.

Dzur, Albert W. 2012. *Punishment, Participatory Democracy and the Jury*. Oxford: Oxford University Press.

Dzur, A.W., and R. Mirchandani. 2007. Punishment and Democracy: The Role of Public Deliberation. *Punishment and Society* 9 (2): 151–175.

Fishkin, James S. 1995. *The Voice of the People: Public Opinion and Democracy*. New Haven: Yale University Press.

Fishkin, J. 1996. Bringing Deliberation to Democracy. *The Public Perspective* 7 (1): 1–4.

Fishkin, J. 2009. *When the People Speak: Deliberative Democracy and Public Consultation*. Oxford: Oxford University Press.

Foucault, Michel. 1991. Governmentality. In *The Foucault Effect: Studies in Governmentality*, ed. G. Burchell, C. Gordon, and P. Miller, 87–104. Chicago: Chicago University Press.

———. 1994. Truth and Juridical Forms. In *Power*, ed. James D. Faubion, 1–9. New York: The New York Press.

Green, David A. 2006. Public Opinion Versus Public Judgment about Crime: Correcting the 'Comedy of Errors'. *British Journal of Criminology* 46: 131–154.
———. 2008. *When Children Kill Children: Penal Populism and Political Culture.* Oxford: Oxford University Press.
Hindelang, M.J. 1974. Public Opinion Regarding Crime, Criminal Justice and Related Topics. *Journal of Research in Crime and Delinquency* 11 (2): 101–116.
Hough, M., and P. Mayhew. 1983. *The British Crime Survey: First Report.* London: Her Majesty's Stationary Office.
Hough, Mike, and Patricia Mayhew. 1985. *Taking Account of Crime: Key Findings From the Second British Crime Survey.* London: Home Office.
Hough, M., H. Lewis, and N. Walker. 1988. Factors Associated with "Punitiveness" in England and Wales. In *Public Attitudes to Sentencing: Surveys from Five Countries*, ed. N. Walker and M. Hough, 203–217. Aldershot: Gower.
Hough, Mike, and Alison Park. 2002. How Malleable are Attitudes to Crime and Punishment? Findings from a British Deliberative Poll. In *Changing Attitudes to Punishment: Public Opinion, Crime and Justice*, ed. J.V. Roberts and M. Hough, 163–183. Cullompton: Willan.
Hough, Mike, and Julian V. Roberts. 1998. *Attitudes to Punishment: Findings from the British Crime Survey.* London: Home Office.
Hughes, J.A., and W.W. Sharrock. 2007. *Theory and Methods in Sociology: An Introduction to Sociological Thinking and Practice.* Basingstoke: Palgrave Macmillan.
Jackson, J., and J. Sunshine. 2007. Public Confidence in Policing: A Neo-Durkheimian Perspective. *British Journal of Criminology* 47 (2): 214–233.
Kendall, G., and G. Whickham. 1999. *Using Foucault's Methods.* London: Sage.
Law, John. 2004. *After Method: Mess in Social Science Research.* Abingdon: Routledge.
Loader, Ian. 2011. Playing with Fire? Democracy and the Emotions of Crime and Punishment. In *Emotions, Crime and Justice*, ed. Susanne Karstedt, Ian Loader, and Heather Strang, 347–362. Oxford: Hart.
Loader, I., and R. Sparks. 2010. Wacquant and Civic Sociology: "Formative Intentions" and Formative Experiences. *Criminology and Criminal Justice* 10 (4): 405–415.
———. 2011. Criminology and Democratic Politics: A Reply to Critics. *British Journal of Criminology* 51 (4): 734–738.
Luskin, Robert C., James S. Fishkin, and Roger Jowell. 2002. Considered Opinions: Deliberative Polling in Britain. *British Journal of Political Science* 32: 455–487.
Mills, C. Wright. 2000. *The Sociological Imagination.* Oxford: Oxford University Press.
Osborne, T., and N. Rose. 1999. Do the Social Sciences Create Phenomena: The Case of Public Opinion Research. *British Journal of Sociology* 50 (3): 367–396.
Pratt, John. 2007. *Penal Populism.* Abingdon: Routledge.

Price, V., and P. Neijens. 1997. Opinion Quality in Public Opinion Research. *International Journal of Public Opinion Research* 9 (4): 336–360.
Roberts, Julian V., and Anthony N. Doob. 1989. Sentencing and Public Opinion: Taking False Shadows for True Substances. *Osgoode Hall Law Journal* 27 (3): 491–503.
Roberts, Julian V., and Mike Hough, eds. 2002. *Changing Attitudes to Punishment: Public Opinion, Crime and Justice*. Cullompton: Willan.
Roberts, Julian V., Loretta J. Stalans, David Indermaur, and Mike Hough. 2003. *Penal Populism and Public Opinion: Lessons from Five Countries*. Oxford: Oxford University Press.
Saward, M. 2003. Enacting Democracy. *Political Studies* 51: 161–179.
Shamir, J., and M. Shamir. 2000. *The Anatomy of Public Opinion*. Michigan: University of Michigan Press.
Smith, Dominic. 2007. *Confidence in the Criminal Justice System: What Lies Beneath?* London: Ministry of Justice.
Van Dijk, J.M. 1979. *The Extent of Public Information and the Nature of Public Attitudes Towards Crime*. Council of Europe Thirteenth Criminological Research Conference: Public Opinion on Crime and Criminal Justice.
Walker, Nigel, and Mike Hough, eds. 1988. *Public Attitudes to Sentencing: Surveys from Five Countries*. Aldershot: Gower.
Williams, M. 1998. The Social World as Knowable. In *Knowing the Social World*, ed. T. May and M. Williams, 5–21. Buckingham: Open University Press.

CHAPTER 4

Archaeology: Surfaces of Emergence for the Public Confidence Agenda

Abstract Turner shows that the shape taken by the public confidence agenda has 'conditions of existence', including the following: (1) increasing separation between the public and the criminal justice system makes it necessary for the public to have confidence in justice, rather than witnessing this first-hand; (2) an understanding of the criminal justice system as legitimately oriented towards the production of effects, which grants 'experts' priority in knowing about and accurately and objectively representing the reality of crime and justice; and (3) a political system which incentivises aspiring political leaders to treat public *perceptions* of policy and practice as centrally important and encourages them to see such perceptions as able to be accurately captured by aggregating opinion surveys. These conditions of existence have emerged through historical changes, including the following: (1) professionalisation of criminal justice limiting opportunities for public participation; (2) a shift towards an instrumental orientation of transforming individuals; and (3) the change to universal adult suffrage creating new expectations for accountability, and, increasingly, managerialist regimes using quantitative performance indicators.

Keywords Foucault, archaeology of knowledge • Penal reform • Genealogy • Modernist criminology • Managerialism • New Public Management • Victimization surveys • British Crime Survey • Left realism • Public confidence in criminal justice

E.R. Turner, *Public Confidence in Criminal Justice*,
Critical Criminological Perspectives,
https://doi.org/10.1007/978-3-319-67897-9_4

The conclusion to Chap. 3 identified some key characteristics of the public confidence agenda. These included the positioning of members of the public as dependent upon experts to understand the reality of crime and justice, the privileging of specialised expert ways of knowing about crime and justice, and the acceptance of generalised survey questions as the most appropriate way to understand how the public think and feel about these issues. The chapter also identified a tendency to elide the value-based decisions underpinning this agenda, as proponents of the aggregative, general, atomised, and passive (AGAP) survey approach presented decisions about 'how to know' as rooted in scientific rather than normative imperatives. In this chapter I show that the shape taken by the public confidence agenda has conditions of existence which rest upon specific historical surfaces of emergence, without which the dominant form of public confidence in criminal justice would be, literally, unthinkable.

The chapter argues that the public confidence agenda is premised on the following conditions of existence: (1) the increasing separation between ordinary members of the public and the operations of the criminal justice system, making it necessary for them to have confidence or belief that it operates in certain ways, rather than witnessing this first-hand; (2) an understanding of the criminal justice system as legitimately oriented towards the production of effects upon individuals facilitated by the existence of experts who are granted priority in knowing about and accurately and objectively representing the reality of crime and justice; and (3) a political system within which members of the public's *perceptions* of policy and practice are treated as centrally important to the operation of the state, and are understood as able to be accurately captured by aggregating opinion surveys.

The surfaces of emergence for these conditions can be found in changes in the way crime is dealt with in England and Wales, occurring over a period of some 400 years. During this time a system of justice emerged which can be differentiated from earlier penal arrangements in three significant ways: (1) managed by a centralised bureaucracy and delivered by professionals, it largely excludes the lay public from participating in or witnessing the administration of punishment and places strict limitations on opportunities for the public to participate in other aspects of criminal justice activity; (2) explicitly oriented to the effective delivery of instrumental ends, it has increasingly come to represent itself as informed by the findings of scientific research and experts of various kinds; (3) funded by compulsory taxpayer contributions, it operates in a society with universal adult suffrage where public institutions are required to be accountable to the public and where managerialist regimes with quantitative performance indicators are used to achieve accountability. In this chapter I provide an overview of these changes and explain how they have provided surfaces of emergence for the idea of public confidence in the criminal justice system.

4.1 Note on Method: Excavating the History of the Present

> I begin with the assumption that the phenomenon to be explained is a present day phenomenon ... and ... my task is to trace its historical conditions of emergence ... and give account of its formation and development. (Lee 2007, 9)

In his 2007 book *Inventing Fear of Crime: Criminology and the Politics of Anxiety*, Lee provided a thought-provoking genealogy of the much-analysed concept of 'fear of crime'. He argued that the will to knowledge, and more specifically the will to 'enumerate' (203), had contributed to the production of a concept which had in turn developed 'its own productive capacities and effects' (134). He described the process of production thus:

> Contingent factors have informed the entire conceptualisation of the fear of crime as an object that might be rendered intelligible through empirical enquiry. ... Fear of crime became an object of governance not because it was "out there", "waiting to be discovered", but because of a number of accidental or contingent discursive alignments or conditions of emergence. (133)

Lee's account of the emergence of the idea of fear of crime offers many illuminating parallels with the story of how public confidence became a prominent object for research and policy, and his approach to his subject matter inspired my own interest in tracing the historical contingencies which allowed the idea of public confidence in the criminal justice system to emerge.

Following the lead of Michel Foucault, genealogical inquiries start from the position that there is 'no necessity at work in history' (Smart 2002, 58). To do genealogy is to seek to understand how an idea (e.g. public confidence) comes to be seen as self-evident and necessary (Smart 2002, 59). The investigative method applied in genealogy was dubbed 'archaeology' by Foucault. A basic component of archaeology entails identifying relationships between 'discursive formations and non-discursive domains (institutions, political events, economic practices and processes)' (Foucault 1972, 179–180).

Archaeology thus aims to uncover the traces of past knowledges, events, and practices which can be identified in contemporary orders of knowledge, and which provide that knowledge with its 'conditions of possibility' (O'Farrall 2005, 63). Foucault's archaeology, then, pivots on the notion that ideas which common sense might be inclined to treat as timeless in fact have a historicity, and that our perspective on these ideas is rooted in the time and place from which we view them (Smart 2002, 58). Indeed, Foucault regarded historical inquiry as the best method for understanding and challenging contemporary regimes of truth (O'Farrall 2005, 54). His analytical focus eschewed the identification of underlying causes of history and instead aimed at uncovering the material conditions which permit certain objects to be thought, and thus to be known (Kendall and Whickham 1999, 35).

Foucault later introduced the idea of 'genealogy': a way of applying his archaeological method to answer present problems by incorporating, along with the historical analysis, an understanding of power. For Foucault, truth was always shaped and organised by power. But undertaking genealogical analysis requires, in the first instance, the application of the archaeological method to uncover how the idea of public confidence (in its dominant contemporary form) became thinkable, that is to say how it was able to emerge as an 'object' for thought. This chapter addresses this task.

4.2 The Removal of Justice from Public View

Four hundred years ago, except for serious crimes, the administration of justice in England was very local and closely tied in to the communities within which people lived out their day-to-day lives. Small and stable communities exercised effective surveillance over their members (Bauman 1987, 42), and, for most people, offences and disputes were settled by the local Court Leet, under the Lord of the Manor (Sharpe 1984, 25). Until the nineteenth century, ordinary members of the public were involved in or able to witness the process of punishment as the sentences passed regularly involved a significant element of public spectacle (Beattie 1986; Foucault 1977). The pillory and the stocks remained available throughout the eighteenth century and effectively left the fate of the offender in the hands of the crowd. Offenders who roused particular anger were treated very roughly, and even killed, whereas those with whom the public felt sympathy often experienced less suffering, and instead received public support, during their period of 'punishment' (Beattie 1986, 466; Emsley 1987, 215).

In London, until 1783, 'the execution march from Newgate prison to Tyburn gallows lasted about two hours, to the accoutrement of tolling bells and all the paraphernalia of spectacle and crowd participation along the way' (Pratt 2002, 16). However, the end of the execution march marked the beginning of 'a trend that involves both restricting the savagery and further confining the spectacle of the execution' (Pratt 2002, 16). In part this trend came about as a result of people turning against some of the more brutal punishments which remained on the statute book, in some cases leading juries to acquit rather than have to submit individuals to the tortures available. For example, in 1794 the shoemaker Thomas Hardy, a founding member of the London Corresponding Society, was acquitted of high treason, an offence which the jury well knew to be punishable by an execution which would include the criminal being disembowelled and castrated whilst still alive (Thompson 1980, 21).

During the nineteenth century, English whipping posts, pillories, stocks, and ducking stools all fell into disuse (Pratt 2002, 15), branding was outlawed (Foucault 1977, 10), public executions were discontinued and recourse to the death penalty declined dramatically (Pratt 2002, 16). Publicly exhibited acts of punishment on the body thus all but disappeared in a change of 'penal style' (Foucault 1977, 7). Furthermore, the kind of informal sanctions which local communities had been accustomed to use to punish minor offenders of accepted morals or custom also declined (Pratt 2002, 16). By the late nineteenth century, ordinary members of the public in England were effectively neither participating in nor witnessing the administration of punishment which became 'the most hidden part of the penal process' (Foucault 1977, 9).

Over the same period, the traditional outlets through which some members of the public might have involved themselves in bringing offenders to justice and determining their sentence were also being closed off or limited. Movements such as the Societies for the Reformation of Manners, which sprang up in the late seventeenth century, only to peter out by about 1730 (see Sharpe 1984), were at odds with the increasingly professionalised and standardised system of justice which started to emerge from the eighteenth century onwards, and which really gathered pace under

Robert Peel at the Home Office during the 1820s (Emsley 1987, 222). The changes progressively reduced and circumscribed opportunities for the public to involve themselves in law enforcement and penal matters, and increasingly posed a challenge to the traditional, paternalistic, aristocratic image of justice based around mercy and discretion, favouring a move towards an 'impersonal justice in which the law was above the suspicion of dependence on any personal discretion' (Emsley 1987, 222).[1]

In line with a wider centralising and rationalising trend in government, the organisation and supervision of prisons increasingly became a matter for the state. The opening of Millbank Prison in 1816 was followed by the founding of the prison inspectorate in 1835, and in 1877 the prison system was centralised under the Home Office establishing an expanding, hierarchically organised and increasingly uniform penal estate (Garland 1990, 181). At the same time, visits into prison by interested members of the public came to be viewed as inappropriate and were increasingly curtailed (Pratt 2002, 55). The role formerly played in inspecting and exposing prison regimes by 'pioneering individuals' and voluntary organisations preaching reform increasingly passed to the state (Pratt 2002, 123).

Until the end of the eighteenth century, the buildings in which prisons were housed tended to look just the same as the ordinary houses next to them (Pratt 2002, 36). But, during the nineteenth century, as prison started to be more frequently used as a penal sanction in its own right, the enlarged prison facilities were removed to outlying areas of towns and cities and situated behind high walls, physically screening their inhabitants from common view (Pratt 2002, 41–45). At the same time, prisoners themselves were publicly exhibited less often, with moves to transport them between penal facilities in civilian clothing rather than prison dress, then in private railway cars, and later in vans (Pratt 2002, 57). Meanwhile, the establishment of professional police forces reduced the extent of popular control over local constables (Reiner 2010, 65). This shift continued in the twentieth century as the 1964 Police Act strengthened the Home Office and Chief Constables at the expense of local police authorities, and the shift to the Unit Beat System of patrol and motorised response meant that the relationship between the 'Bobby' and a local community was further loosened (Reiner 2010, 79).

Between the seventeenth and twentieth centuries, then, the public were increasingly deprived of the channels through which they had been accustomed to being involved in, or at least physically witnessing, the processes in place for enforcing laws and punishing wrong doers (cf. Garland 1990, 185). As the machinery of punishment was progressively removed from public view, and as responsibility for preventing crime and apprehending offenders passed to professional police, so the public were no longer able to 'see for themselves' justice being done. Now they must rely instead on the information released from within the bureaucracy, and on official assurances that the appropriate action has been taken to apprehend individuals who commit crime and punish them. This gradual exclusion of the public provided a surface of emergence for the contemporary idea of public confidence because it made it necessary for members of the public to rely on the testimony of others to find out how the criminal justice system was operating.

4.3 The Move Towards an Emphasis on Instrumental Goals in Penality

The need to provide a deterrent to crime has been a justification of the right to punish for centuries, albeit a justification which was, at least until the nineteenth century, used in support of the public exhibition of torture and death (Foucault 1977, 93). Beattie (1986, 469) notes that public corporal punishment was supposed 'to discourage [the offender] and others from committing other offenses. And beyond that ... performed the wider function of reaffirming the moral boundaries of the society.' Some would argue that the existence of broader correctional intentions towards the individual offender (as opposed to the use of their bodily suffering as a deterrent example) also has a long history. In the late fifteenth century, Edward VI bequeathed a former palace (Bridewell) to the city of London as 'a workhouse for the poor and idle persons of the city' (Salgādo 1977, 189). The palace came to be used as both a hospital and a 'house of correction' for rogues and loose women who were sent there for 'reformatory detention' *after* receiving the punishment prescribed by the court. Reform was to be achieved at Bridewell by putting the inmates to useful work under the supervision of paid craftspeople (Salgādo 1977, 190).

The 1572 Poor Law saw a system modelled on Bridewell being adopted around the country, with the aim of ensuring that potentially wayward youths grew up engaged in hard work. The law gave parishes the power to round up obvious vagrants and to punish those resistant to working by whipping them and withholding their food (Salgādo 1977, 196–7). Further statutes permitted the imposition of a period in this kind of house of correction *in addition to* the ordinary punishment. With objectives which extended beyond retributive punishment and the deterrence of would-be criminals, Bridewell and related institutions can be, and have been, interpreted as prototypical correctional institutions. Their existence during the fifteenth and sixteenth centuries appears to demonstrate the early prevalence of the idea that 'it might be possible to cure criminal instincts though a healthy dose of labour discipline' (Sharpe 1984, 179). However, these apparently 'correctionalist' practices existed in a quite different social context than later practices which aimed specifically to change offenders' behaviour, and it may be misleading to suggest that there is a straightforward continuity here.

Bauman's work on the emergence of modern 'experts' suggests an alternative interpretation of Bridewell and the early correctional institutions. In sixteenth-century England, social and economic changes were afoot which broke up settled feudal communities and made increasing numbers of men and women 'economically redundant, and consequently socially homeless' (Bauman 1987, 40). Anonymous, mobile, and with no legitimate means of providing for their own survival, these homeless individuals were viewed with fear and suspicion, but, as they moved from place to place, they were effectively invisible to traditional forms of surveillance carried out by the community. This shortfall of surveillance was to be filled by the state, a development which, according to Bauman, transformed the exercise of disciplinary power into something 'visible, a problem to be taken care of, something to be designed for, organized, managed and consciously attended to' (Bauman 1987, 42).

As the first movement in the process of re-establishing surveillance, the state sought to define 'vagabondage' and, in 1531, passed an act of parliament which settled on a definition which made 'possession of a master or a property … the conditions of normal non-punishable conduct' (43). The solution to the state of vagabondage was thus identified as the restoration of authority over the individual. In 1569 the Privy Council ordered parish constables to carry out a search which identified 13,000 'rogues and masterless men' roaming the country (Salgādo 1977, vii). Seen in this light the early houses of correction seem to be less about correcting the *behaviour* of individuals, and more about correcting their *condition*, by putting them to work under a master. The quantification of the problem also reveals the desire of the state to make vagabonds, who, by virtue of their rootlessness, were invisible to effective community surveillance, visible in another way, a theme which found a most clear and brutal expression in the introduction of branding in 1604 (Bauman 1987, 44).

The vagabondage laws represented an important juncture in the shift from surveillance within the community to surveillance by the state, a shift furthered by the widespread use of 'enforced confinement' (Bauman 1987, 44) to deal with problematic individuals existing outside of traditional social structures. Bauman suggests that

> prisons, workhouses, poorhouses, hospitals, mental asylums, were all by-products of the same powerful thrust to render the obscure transparent, to design conditions for redeploying the method of control-through-surveillance once the conditions of its traditional deployment proved increasingly ineffective. (1987, 45)

This shift introduced 'an asymmetry of control' (Bauman 1987, 46), whereby surveillance lost its previous quality of reciprocity: 'the watchers' were now to be permanently distinguished from 'the watched' with surveillance flowing only in one direction. This 'unidirectional' surveillance was to develop into the 'objectivization' of individuals in order that they could be categorised and thus subjected to statistical analysis (Bauman 1987, 47). Furthermore, the conversion to asymmetrical surveillance tended towards the production of an occupational specialism: the 'surveillor' became a dedicated professional and their task more ambitious: 'nothing less than a total reshaping of human behavioural patterns; an imposition of a uniform bodily rhythm upon the variegated inclinations of many individuals; a transformation of a collection of motivated subjects into a category of uniform objects' (Bauman 1987, 48).

So, early houses of correction were engaged less in *producing* effects (instrumentality) than they were in *being* effects in themselves. However, they were part of a regime which played a crucial role in the transformation of surveillance, permitting the development of new forms of expertise. Eventually these forms of expertise would provide knowledge to underpin a criminal justice system which perceived and represented itself as pursuing instrumental objectives, including the transformation of offenders into law-abiding citizens, through the application of 'expert' knowledge. However, that is racing ahead and I wish to return to some other aspects of instrumentality which existed in earlier centuries.

Although it might not yet have had as its objective the transformation of the individual offender, sixteenth- and seventeenth-century penality did, as mentioned above, understand and represent itself as acting as a deterrent to criminality. Furthermore, for more serious offences, the courts could incapacitate offenders by passing the death penalty for a wide range of what we might now consider relatively minor offences. In fact, until the eighteenth century, most offenders convicted at the assizes court were guilty of treason or a felony and so the only available sentence was death (Beattie 1986, 450). However, as described above, hundreds of such convicts could escape the death sentence by pleading 'benefit of clergy'. The lack of choice available to judges in capital cases was, by the second half of the seventeenth century, increasingly seen as a problem, and attempts were being made to make a wider range of options available (Beattie 1986, 450).

The formal introduction of penal transportation to the American colonies in 1718 provided judges with such an alternative. Transportation of convicts was already in use before this time, usually as a condition of pardon, and, Beattie (1986, 472–3) argues, was carried out in

> the hope and expectation that men who had lost their characters in England might well become productive citizens in a new society, that the harsh discipline of the raw society across the Atlantic would reclaim men from the laziness and the bad habits that it was assumed had gradually led them into crime in the first place. The rehabilitation of offenders was not a major consideration in the seventeenth century, but it was obviously recognized as a secondary advantage of transportation.

This suggests the existence of a desire for offenders to be reformed by their punishment, albeit a desire based on 'hope', at best 'expectation'.

Many viewed penal transportation favourably, as it removed offenders physically to another place for a significant period of time, and if they continued offending after their punishment was at an end, most of them were doing it somewhere else.[2] The instrumental 'effectiveness' of this sanction was, then, self-evident. However, transportation was also given a correctionalist spin by the House of Commons Committee on Transportation which, in 1784, suggested that transportation to the American colonies tended to 'reclaim the Objects on which it was inflicted, and to render them good Citizens' (Emsley 1987, 218). There was long-standing scepticism about the potential for imprisonment to achieve similar objectives.

In 1621, a draft bill presented to parliament expressed concern that prison did not make offenders less likely to cause problems upon their release:

> long imprisonment in common gaoles rendreth such offenders the more obdurate and desperate when they are delivered out of the gaoles, they being then poor, miserable, and friendless, are in a manner exposed to the

> like mischiefs, they not having means of their owne, nor place of habitation nor likely to gain so much credit from any honest householder to interteyn them. (Cited in Sharpe 1984, 182)

However, during the seventeenth century, we begin to see houses of correction, as opposed to 'common gaoles', referred to as being able to bring about a change in individuals who would then behave better on the 'outside'.[3] During the eighteenth century, Bridewell itself was still disparagingly referred to as 'a nursery for thieves and prostitutes' (Hanway 1775, 72 cited in Emsley 1987, 218).

In 1779, Parliament passed the Penitentiary Act providing for the construction of two penitentiaries within which inmates would be uniformed, would engage in hard labour during the day, and would be shut in solitary confinement at night. The act specifically stated that these institutions should produce 'habits of Industry' in the prisoners, but also that the regime should be sufficiently harsh as to minimise its appeal to impoverished people (Emsley 1987, 217–8). The institutions were never built, but the Penitentiary Act provides an example of an explicit attempt to produce particular effects on people through punishment: prisoners were to gain particular 'habits' during their sentence but were not to be so well treated that their situation might appear enviable.

It seems, then, that the desire for penal policy to serve a purpose has long played a part in English penal debates. However, changes have occurred in the way in which 'effectiveness' is conceptualised and in the manner of the identification and justification of practices to produce effects. By the end of the eighteenth century, the effect of penal practices *upon the individual offender* was increasingly a matter for discussion. One reason for this might be that, following the significant reduction in the use of execution during the seventeenth century (Beattie 1986, 469), and interruptions to the use of transportation during the eighteenth, there were periods when many offenders guilty of felonies were no longer stopped from offending in England by the simple expedients of killing them, or permanently removing them to a faraway place.

Additionally, intensified anxiety about disorder and criminality amongst the propertied classes in eighteenth-century England (developed against the backdrop of the French Revolution and smaller, but perhaps no less frightening, domestic disturbances, as well as more mundane offending such as highway robbery) precipitated a growing sense of the urgent need to 'govern criminal offending' (Lee 2007, 27). The knowledge that such offenders were simply being imprisoned for a period before being released back into contact with the law-abiding population is likely to have concentrated minds on how those individuals might be reclaimed as good citizens.

4.4 *Homo criminalis* and 'The Science of the State': The Coming of Criminology

The desire to gain a more effective and extensive level of control over citizens played an important part in the construction of eighteenth-century arguments for penal reform. Those in favour of reform were not so much concerned that the use of spectacular public torture as punishment was *cruel* as that it was *ineffective*. The desire to make punishment 'an art of effects' (Foucault 1977, 93) underpinned the emergence of Enlightenment-inspired classical criminological thought during the eighteenth century, and the attempt to identify more 'rational' approaches to governing crime and punishment. In the British context, brothers Henry and John Fielding, and, later, Patrick Colquhoun, were busy developing blueprints for policing and disciplining the lower classes (Lee 2007, 28–31). However, whereas references to criminals in earlier centuries had been infused with loathing and had focused on the need to visit harsh punishment and privations upon their persons and forcibly change their 'habits', by the end of the nineteenth century the language was starting to shift towards a rationalistic objective discourse which began to humanise the figure of the criminal as an individual towards whom the state has responsibilities (Pratt 2002, 86–9).

Whether the intentions were humanitarian or repressive, the crucial element of this shift was that justice was no longer a matter of punishing *the offence* but was also something which was targeted at *the offender*. To the 'triangle' of classical criminology—law, crime, and punishment—was added the figure of the criminal: '*homo criminalis*' (Pasquino 1991, 237–8). Sentences were now supposed to address this figure, his thoughts, instincts, drives and tendencies, and include measures 'to supervise the individual, neutralize his dangerous state of mind, to alter his criminal tendencies and to continue even when this change has been achieved' (Foucault 1977, 18). That such a shift could occur was, according to Foucault (18), attributable to the way in which 'scientific' expertise inserted itself into a crack in the legislation and expanded over time to provide a battery of 'knowledges, techniques [and] "scientific" discourses' upon which judgment must now be based'. Developments in post-revolutionary France are instructive. Legislators found that the tenets of strict classicism were occasionally problematic because some offenders could not understand the charge against them. Thus, specialist expert witnesses entered into legal proceedings to attest to the capability of individuals (Foucault, 1977).

This approach brought to the fore the idea that there might be factors which pre-disposed people to commit crimes (Hopkins-Burke 2009, 24, 31–2). The object of judgement was thus no longer merely the act which had been committed, but also the 'soul' of the perpetrator, creating new possibilities for juridical power:

> by solemnly inscribing offences in the field of objects susceptible of scientific knowledge, they provide the mechanisms of legal punishment with a justifiable hold not only on offences, but on individuals; not only on what they do, but also on what they are, will be, may be. (Foucault 1977, 18)

The 'scientific' discourses of 'experts' thus came to permeate a system of criminal justice which 'functions and justifies itself only by this perpetual reference to something other than itself, by this unceasing reinscription in non-juridical systems' (22).

Following the economic transition to capitalism and the relinquishing of notions of sociality rooted in the old feudal order, individuals were no longer required to live their lives in a certain condition (under one master, in one place), but were required to have certain dispositions and take (or refrain from taking) certain actions. Where early correctionalist moves sought to restore individual vagabonds to the lawful condition of having a master (see above), now correctionalism must have another objective: to create the right kinds of people. The increasingly professionalised mechanisms of surveillance identified by Bauman (see above) could thus be put to work to categorise and monitor individuals and to begin to enquire into the workings of their 'soul'.

The new 'scientific' discourse which emerged in the modern era was oriented to these new objectives with statistics (or 'the science of the state') being linked to a new approach to the 'art of government' (Foucault 1991, 96). Whilst numbers had been collected and recorded at early stages in the modern period, Hacking (1991) has argued that during the nineteenth century there occurred both a quantitative and a qualitative shift in the use of numbers. Quantitatively, between 1820 and 1840 he suggests there was a rapid expansion in the publication of numerical information and that an 'avalanche of numbers ... revealed an astonishing regularity'

(187). Qualitatively, there were shifts in the understanding, interpretation and use of these numbers: 'Where in 1800 chance had been nothing real, at the end of the century it was something "real" precisely because one had found the form of laws that were to govern chance' (185). Statistical calculation was found to be applicable to the practical problems of the day. For example, in the early nineteenth century, Friendly Societies wishing to provide assurance protection to working people were able to calculate the level at which they should set their premiums, and thus: '[t]here arose a certain style of solving practical problems by the collection of data. Nobody argued for this style; they merely found themselves practising it' (192).

Under this shift, this taming of chance, the notion of 'expertise' gained a new meaning. In the sixteenth century, pamphlet writers gave advice on how law-abiding folk could avoid falling prey to 'conycatchers' (thieves and tricksters), with their claims to expertise resting on their position as Justices of the Peace with significant direct experience of dealing with such 'villains' (See Salgādo 1977, 8). By the nineteenth century, rather than needing to have such direct practical experience of the phenomenon in question, experts could now quantify and illuminate phenomena at the level of population by way of mastery and application of the appropriate techniques (Foucault 1991, 99). In this way, 'hitherto invisible processes and phenomena were made calculable and knowable and new modes of government rendered possible' (Lee 2007, 38).

By the end of the nineteenth century, scientific criminology and penology had emerged in Europe and North America bringing a 'rationalization' of penal discourse and an orientation towards technical methods for controlling crime. Criminology was 'an expression of the Enlightenment ambition to cure social ills by the application of Reason', and, according to this view, the expert was an essential part of finding solutions to the problem of crime (Garland 1990, 185). This change was internalised in the self-representations of criminal justice professionals: 'Instead of being the vehicles of punitive reaction … these groups tend to represent themselves positively, as technicians of reform, as social work professionals, or as institutional managers' (Garland 1990, 182–3). After 1945, penal discourse increasingly focused on the provision of rehabilitation, assistance, and therapeutic interventions for the offender, with a basis in psychological/psychiatric expertise (Pratt 2002, 91–4). Garland suggests, 'If we nowadays expect "results" from punishing, it is in large part the doing of these groups and their self-descriptions' (Garland 1990, 183).

4.5 'Justice Tempered by Understanding': Modern Criminology in Britain

In the twentieth century, the decades following the Second World War were decisive in establishing sites of technical criminological expertise which could be used to inform penal practice in England and Wales. In 1944, a report for the Home Office recommended that studies should be made of 'the effectiveness of penal treatment, recidivism, the value of approved school training, the personality of offenders, the criteria used by the police in recording crime, and the efficiency of probation officers' (Lodge 1974, 14). Following on from this recommendation, the Home Office Research Unit was formed in 1957[4] and the Cambridge Institute of Criminology in 1959.

Looking back on these formative years for English criminology Lord Butler recalls that, as Home Secretary at the time, he was attempting to 'lay a path for an enlightened penal policy' (Butler 1974, 1). He continued:

> Crime and its treatment seem to me to be no less suitable as a subject for study and teaching by the universities than a number of other social phenomena; and this is a field in which we particularly need the help and urge of the informed but detached public opinion which the universities are so well able to produce. (4–5)

The so-called founding fathers of criminology who were establishing themselves in this period cleaved to the belief that the knowledge which they produced would inform improved criminal justice policies (Tonry and Green 2003, 500).

These changes were contiguous with the prevailing mood in government, with the state's involvement in sponsoring criminological research from the late 1950s onwards appearing to be 'part-and-parcel of the generally more interventionist state' (Reiner 2010, 147), and with the rehabilitative ideal being in large part a reflection of a high level of optimism about the potential of scientific knowledge to guide positive social change (Tonry and Green 2003, 507). Furthermore, there appears to have been support both within government and within the legal profession for closer relations between the social sciences and law, in order that empirically generated social scientific insights might be used to deliver 'justice tempered by understanding' (Ormrod 1964, 331). The type of 'understanding' referred to here is quite specific: 'understanding' was to be generated through scientific research into the causes of and remedies for criminality. What has been described as an 'emphatically modern' criminological discourse is thus characterised by 'its faith in instrumental reason, its vision of the technocratic state and its commitment to social progress and social engineering' (Garland and Sparks 2000, 8).

Over a period of about 200 years then (although arguably set in train by conditions which emerged during earlier periods), a new source of authority emerged in relation to criminal justice: 'Expertise in the conduct of conduct – authority arising out of a claim to a true and positive knowledge of humans, to neutrality and to efficacy' (Rose 1993, 284). The most salient effect of this, for our purposes in this book, is its tendency to exclude and devalue other forms of knowledge. As an example of this, in relation to the death penalty, a penal sanction which a majority of the public have persisted in supporting 'the growth of penological evidence ... not only discredited deterrence and retribution arguments, but increasingly emphasised the importance of treatment and rehabilitation' (Pratt 2002, 29), such that in the 1950s, scientific evidence was deployed as a way of bolstering calls for the abolition of the death penalty (28). This move indicated a willingness to prioritise 'scientific', 'rational' knowledge over public opinion, such that 'the state was prepared to exert its own moral authority to govern in this area, and to place the way it punished its subjects above political interests and populist demands' (32–3). Penal experts were thus united by the view that 'public opinion...was something to be wary of, not to be trusted, allowing as it did sentiments of anger and uncontrolled emotion to blind it to more rational thinking' (32).

Between the sixteenth and twentieth centuries, then, shifts in understandings of criminal justice, and in ways of knowing about populations, supported the emergence of the notion that the criminal justice system should be oriented to the production of effects within those individuals subject to its discipline. An emerging set of experts began to make claims to be able to accurately and objectively know and represent the reality of crime, justice, and the effects of different penal sanctions using modern scientific techniques. The type of knowledge about crime, criminality, and justice which could be gained through personal experience was henceforth to be regarded as, at best, an adjunct to scientific knowledge oriented towards instrumental ends.

In reflecting on the emergence of modern society, Giddens (1990, 22) argues that the process occurred through two 'disembedding mechanisms': 'symbolic tokens' and 'expert systems'. Both of these serve to 'stretch' social systems: our expectations are no longer rooted in localised, personal, chronologically coincident relationships (28). They reflect impersonal at-a-distance associations which are reliant upon trust not in the individual persons involved, but in 'abstract capacities' (26). Giddens sees trust as a specific form of confidence, and as particularly pertinent in conditions where people lack full information (33). Trust links together faith and confidence and reflects 'confidence in the reliability of a person or system, regarding a given set of outcomes or events' which can be seen as faith in '*the correctness of abstract principles*' (34, emphasis added).

The removal of criminal justice processes from public view, the exclusion of the public from taking part in such processes, and the reorientation towards the production of instrumental effects can all be understood as part of the movement towards a *modern* criminal justice system, 'disembedded' from society by becoming an 'expert system'. Such a system is reliant upon public trust in the 'abstract principles' according to which it is organised, in this case the idea that the science of criminology can inform and evaluate the operation of justice. The problem of public confidence, then, is a particularly modern problem, intimately associated with broader issues of trust in experts and the rules they abide by in producing knowledge. It becomes a matter of acute concern when full adult suffrage and the intensification of electoral conflict create conditions where confidence itself becomes an object for scientific study and managerial control.

4.6 Bringing the Public Back in: From Full Adult Suffrage to Managerialist Accountability via the (Re)invention of 'Public Opinion'

Democracy, and the advent of full adult suffrage, contributed to a new set of 'problems of collective judgement and decision making', promoting the development of new empirical methods for capturing and representing the 'opinions' of the public (Price and Neijens 1997, 339). Speaking at the first conference on Attitude and Opinion Research in 1949, Samuel Stouffer of Harvard University Division of Social Relations described polling as an 'instrument of democracy' (Lee 2007, 50). The development and expansion of opinion polling offered a new way of knowing about and understanding what individual members of the public thought about different issues of the day. The notion of public opinion as we know it today was effectively brought into being as mass survey data came to be seen as 'the only workable empirical rendering of public opinion' (Price and Neijens 1997, 336).

Criminologists began taking more of an interest in the opinions of members of the public from the 1970s onwards, particularly through the increasing use of victimisation surveys as a method for understanding the crime problem as experienced by more vulnerable and disadvantaged groups, including women, ethnic minorities, and working-class communities. Victimisation surveys first emerged in the US when it was recognised that recorded crime figures indicated that a disproportionate burden of crime was borne by the poor and ethnic minority residents of the urban 'ghetto', and when feminist 'victimology' was determined to raise awareness of the hidden crimes suffered by women (Jones et al. 1986).

The first three US victimisation surveys (carried out for the President's Commission in the late 1960s) inspired many subsequent surveys in the US and beyond, as well as the formation of a body to take forwards work on a National Crime Survey (NCS), which commenced in 1972. Despite some identified methodological shortcomings[5], throughout the 1970s the new data on victimisation made a 'substantial impact' in academic criminological circles (Sparks 1981, 5), providing as a matter of routine a 'wealth of data ... on a range of crime-related topics' about which virtually nothing had been known less than a decade earlier (24). Initially, the NCS and other victimisation studies were intended mainly as a way of obtaining more accurate estimations of the levels of different types of crime, and how they impacted on different groups (7). In fulfilling this role, they presented data which revealed *inter alia* that most crime is not reported, that incidents of violent victimisation are generally extremely rare, that a small number of repeatedly victimised individuals suffer a high impact from crime, that certain groups have a significantly higher level of risk of victimisation than others, and, crucially, that criminal victimisation frequently takes place *within* rather than *between* different social classes (Sparks 1981).

Revelations about the extent of intra-class crime and the scale of working-class victimisation proved particularly problematic for radical criminologists who had tended to downplay or ignore these aspects of criminal behaviour (Young 1988, 171). In response to what they regarded as the empirical exposure of radical criminology's blind spots, the new 'left realist' criminologists sought to provide a middle way between establishment criminology and what they termed the 'left idealism' of radical criminology. This middle way would 'take crime seriously', particularly its impact on the lived experiences of working-class people, and it would seek to offer greater practical support to mainstream politicians of the left who were seeking policies which would be both advantageous and attractive to their core constituency. It would also provide radical analysis and policy alternatives (Young 1997, 474). The 'left realist' movement thus combined empirical and political objectives.

Later, second-generation victimisation studies moved on from simply quantifying the extent of victimisation. They included additional variables intended to gauge respondents' assessments of responses to crime by the police and other criminal justice agencies. The scope of the victimisation survey was thus expanded to 'embrace a much greater part of the whole process of criminalization – namely, the pattern of victimization, the impact of crime, the actual police response and the public's notions of appropriate penalties for various offences' (Jones et al. 1986, 5). This extended focus meant that victimisation surveys could provide the kind of empirical data which was considered crucial by left realists: 'The virtue ... of a crime survey is that it provides us with a more realistic mapping of the impact of crime and policing, and it also reminds us that we should take seriously people's knowledge of crime' (201). Furthermore, left realists argued that 'being tough on crime must include being tough on the criminal justice system' (Young 1997, 491). Local victimisation surveys were a mechanism through which crime control interventions could be monitored, and agencies held to account via a regular 'audit of people's experiences, anxieties and problems of crime' (Jones et al. 1986, 3).

The early 1980s saw the Islington, Merseyside, and Nottinghamshire Crime Surveys, with the last two being directly encouraged and funded by the Home Office. These local surveys were rather different in scope to the national-scale BCS, which was then just getting off the ground. The local studies focused on specific urban localities—those containing the highest concentrations of poor and marginalised individuals (White and Haines 2008, 148–151)—and produced reports which would have made uncomfortable reading for many within the criminal justice system, particularly some senior police officers.

The Islington Crime Survey found 'widespread public scepticism about the ability of the police to combat the crimes which are of the greatest public concern' (Jones et al. 1986, 203). It also highlighted the fact that a significant proportion of the local population believed that the police acted illegally and unfairly towards certain groups, basing this belief, they said, on their own experience or the experiences of friends. The authors highlighted the potential impacts of such a belief, including reduced cooperation of the public with the police and an increasing likelihood that certain groups may be propelled towards delinquency (205). As a result, they recommended: 'In order to increase information flow it is essential that the police gain the confidence of the public' (213).

In their recommendations, the authors referred to the types of police action which would command public support, and they contrasted senior officers' assumptions about 'what the public want' with the 'reality' identified by the survey. Finally, they argued that there was a need to construct effective performance indicators based on community priorities: 'it is paramount that the public gets value for money. For this reason it is necessary to develop a series of performance indicators which are independently audited. With this in mind the regular crime survey is a useful tool into which can be built the relevant indicators' (211). The indicators suggested included 'public satisfaction with requests for police assistance'.

In championing the use of local crime surveys, situating crime in relation to wider harms and social issues, and foregrounding the lived experiences, feelings, and perceptions of members of the public, the left realist criminological perspective provided a framework which was subsequently developed under the auspices of 'community safety' during the 1980s and 1990s (Squires 1997). As Squires (1997, 8) notes: 'the new service culture required new methods of discovering what the public "really wanted."' Local crime surveys were one mechanism through which this could be achieved and, as such, there is a link between the left realist perspective in criminology and the development of a quantitatively oriented, perception-focused managerialist framework within criminal justice. There is an irony in the way managerialism and community safety collided: the methods of managerialism, particularly the focus on measurement, may have worked to undermine some of the ethos of community safety. By judging community safety based on public perceptions measured through surveys much community safety work turned towards 'image management' (15) and members of communities were increasingly understood as consumers of community safety and criminal justice services: 'the real "prize" at stake in the consumer culture and behind the new managerialist initiatives is the rebuilding of public confidence and the attempted resurrection of "policing by consent"' (8).

However, the 1980s saw a curtailment of ambition and scope in local crime surveys in England and Wales. The local surveys appear to have suffered the same fate as those in the US, where local victimisation surveys tailed off in number after the early 1970s, almost certainly due to the existence of the massive NCS (Sparks 1981, 11). The first national-scale BCS was planned and carried out under the supervision of the internal Home Office research unit in the early 1980s. The first report on the BCS, Home Office Research Study (HORS) 76, published in 1983, explicitly claimed that public reactions to their experiences and expectations of the criminal justice system were of vital importance to how well the system could operate because 'any democratic system of law needs the consent of those whom it polices' (Hough and Mayhew 1983, 28). As described in the previous two chapters, at this time Home Office researchers, cognisant of political concern about levels of public support for criminal justice agencies, began to make claims about the need to be able to 'gauge' public confidence.

The British model may have been influenced by developments in the US, where, during the 1970s, social researchers started to write about how existing opinion poll data might be used by policymakers to shape their actions around criminal justice issues. The 'Application of Victimization Survey Results' project had the explicit aim of using the data from the National Crime Survey, begun in 1972 'to examine issues that have particular relevance for applications to the immediate needs of operational criminal justice programs' (Garofalo 1977, 3). Those involved with the programme made the following claims.

> Little systematic attention has been given to a growing body of public opinion surveys which have potential as barometers of public sentiment...the results of these surveys may be useful in attempts to understand the behaviour of Americans with regard to crime-related topics and the differential responses of segments of American society to aspects of the criminal justice system; further, knowledge of the opinions of Americans on topics related to criminal justice may illuminate the public's moods and priorities ... and may also foreshadow impending popular pressure for legislative changes. (Hindelang 1974, 101)

> An understanding of the areas examined ... is important if criminal justice programs are to integrate public opinion into their planning process: sensitivity to public opinion is a key to success for any criminal justice program. Public attitudes about crime, then, constitute an important topic for study in modern criminal justice'. (Garofalo 1977, 13)

These claims appear to have been heeded, and to have reverberated, over the years, and across the Atlantic Ocean.

At the same time as the BCS was getting established, a shift towards neoliberal modes of governing was increasing the emphasis placed on the accountability and efficiency of public services (O'Malley 1999, 180) and service delivery was increasingly being organised along 'New Public Management' (NPM) lines (Fielding and Innes 2006, 131; Hood 1991; Hough 2003; Young and Matthews 2003, 2). Garland (1996, 456) suggests that this new managerial ethos in the criminal justice system entailed a redefinition of the mission of state agencies in terms of 'serving particular "consumers"... and being responsive to their expressed needs, rather than serving the more abstract, top-down notion of the public good' (see also Bottoms 1995). This shift, along with NPM's insistence on the use of quantitative success indicators to measure and manage performance meant a growth in 'the practice of conducting surveys of the views of consumers and the development of objectives and priorities which seek to respond to these' (Garland 1996, 456). Hough (2003, 149) argued that the introduction of managerialist logics within the criminal justice system may have had the unintended consequence of reducing confidence in the police and the judiciary, a problem which, he argued, required urgent attention and more resources than were available at the time of writing.

The managerialist trend in public policy can be understood as a key aspect of the rise in neoliberal approaches to governance. Although it is acknowledged that in practice 'neoliberalism' does not conform to an overarching theory (Bell 2011, 140–1), there are certain characteristics which are core to understanding its political logic and social effects. The tendency to (re)imagine and actively seek to (re)constitute the citizen as the self-interested individual consumer of government-funded goods and services is a key facet of the neoliberal outlook. This conception of the citizen is hostile territory for the deliberative understanding of public opinion as a phenomenon formed and expressed in the context of social interaction. It is, as will be discussed in more detail in Chap. 6, a conception of the citizen which simultaneously reflects and reinforces a political culture within which mass survey data is regarded as 'the only workable empirical rendering of public opinion' (Price and Neijens 1997, 336).

Both Left Realist criminology and the change in the management of public services, then, contributed to the production of an enlarged body of knowledge about public perceptions of the criminal justice system, and encouraged, if not required, criminal justice practitioners to gauge the adequacy of their services with respect to public perceptions of those services. The empirical focus on how the experience of victimisation impacts on the lives of different groups within society, the insistence on exploring what the public think, feel, and believe about crime and the criminal justice system, and the explicit attempts to bind together victimisation research and performance measurement of the criminal justice system all supported the construction of the public confidence agenda.

4.7 Conclusion

This historical overview has (hopefully) illustrated the point that, as the public were increasingly excluded from participating in or witnessing key aspects of criminal justice, a new form of 'expert' knowledge emerged which impeded the public themselves from being allowed to 'know' the 'true' reality of crime without expert assistance. Technical knowledge and the use of (ostensibly) morally neutral classifications and typologies to fit offenders to regimes came to displace or to disguise any moral element in punishment (Garland 1990, 187). Whereas in earlier periods attempts to reform offenders were based on 'hope' and 'expectations', by the second part of the twentieth century policy was made based on a belief that the true effectiveness of penal sanctions could now be measured (Hacking 1991, 187). The use of techniques of probability fixed the analytical focus on statistical regularity, and excluded non-experts from being able to 'know' what was 'really' going on. As a result, ordinary members of the public can no longer 'know' but must instead trust in the 'abstract principles' underpinning the production of scientific facts that are meant to support 'confidence' that the criminal justice system is effective.

By the mid-twentieth century, the views of the public were increasingly sought out and captured by a growing opinion polling industry. Acceptance of the need for government action to be 'in tune' (or at least not too far out of tune) with the sentiments of the people meant that more than ever before organisations were asking the public to give an opinion on criminal justice matters. As those opinions were increasingly communicated to, and used by, politicians and the media, opinion polls came to be seen as the most natural and legitimate mechanisms for capturing public views. The very existence of the opinion polling industry implied that the public *should* be asked for their opinion and that their opinions could be captured.

Towards the end of the twentieth century, a new movement in criminology—'left realism'—appropriated and utilised some of the techniques of the polling industry to build a body of criminological knowledge which was rooted in ordinary people's experiences of crime. Left realists argued that the criminal justice system should be more accountable to the public, and the coincidence between this call for accountability and a growing trend for the use of quantitative performance indicators under the New Public Management have left a legacy of large-scale quantitative data and research projects providing information on what the public think about crime and criminal justice.

The contemporary discourse of public confidence in the criminal justice system had specific conditions of existence without which it would not have become thinkable. The contemporary 'problem' of public confidence in the criminal justice system could not exist unless the public had been progressively excluded from a professionalised 'expert system' for dealing with criminal deviance, and had their accustomed ways of knowing about crime and justice not been increasingly discredited by new groups of 'experts', applying new 'modern' ways of knowing. Under these conditions, most members of the public no longer have direct personal access to the 'reality' of crime and punishment and thus must instead trust in the 'expert system' (Giddens 1990, 22) which assumes the role of accurately describing 'reality'. Thus, the idea of public confidence in criminal justice in its late twentieth-century incarnation was always about the 'gap' between 'expert' and 'lay' ways of knowing that opened up over the previous 400 years.

In liberal democratic societies, the 'opinions' of members of the public must be seen to count for something when policies are made and enacted for and upon them. And during the twentieth century, mechanisms were devised to measure those opinions, mechanisms that have been adopted by researchers to 'measure' public confidence (or so they claim). These 'surfaces of emergence' made it *possible* for the contemporary discourse of public confidence in the criminal justice system to emerge; however, they do not adequately explain *how* it emerged. This will be explored in the next chapter.

Notes

1. This trend can also be seen in the demise of the practice of 'pleading benefit of clergy', which allowed hundreds of offenders each year to escape hanging for minor offences against property in what 'amounted in fact to a

pre-sentencing pardoning system' which rested upon the clergyman's willingness to attest to the ability of the illiterate to read, and the judge's willingness to participate in the fiction (Beattie 1986, 474). This historical anomaly, which resulted in some capital offenders receiving the relatively mild (for the time) punishment of branding to the thumb, was addressed in the mid-seventeenth century by the introduction of pardons conditional on accepting transportation. Once judges had a merciful alternative to execution, they were less willing to permit a plea for 'benefit of clergy' (Beattie 1986, 474–5). Judicial discretion was thus increased by the demise of this practice, but the clergy were no longer involved in any collusion to produce mercy.

2. For example, in 1786 the Lord Mayor and Aldermen of the City of London petitioned the king about the rising tide of crime which they considered to be attributable to the end of transportation meaning that offenders who had served their sentence were now being released in England (at that time transportation to America had been ended due to the war of independence) (Emsley 1987: 218). The following year the first convicts departed for Botany Bay (Emsley 1987, 203). It is also instructive to recall at this stage the link between economic redundancy, social homelessness, and perceived criminality, referred to above, and also to note that transportation to America, and later Australia, was used both as a legally inscribed penal sanction, *and* as a way of disposing of surplus peasant populations (most notoriously from Ireland and the Scottish Highlands). At various stages between the sixteenth and nineteenth centuries (depending on geographic location), vast numbers of peasants found themselves surplus to the requirements of landlords and forcibly dispossessed of both the right of access to common land, and the right to cultivate land suitable for maintaining their subsistence. In becoming thus both 'masterless' and deprived of legitimate ways of obtaining the means of existence, they were exposed to the risk of severe destitution and starvation, which may have led them into courses of action where they would fall foul of the criminal law. Either way, enforced emigration or penal transportation were available to dispose of them, ostensibly to improve their situation, but certainly furthering the aims of the landed gentry to extract maximum rent from their land, as well as assisting the government in populating its new overseas possessions (Prebble 1969; Hill 1972; Thompson 1980; Hunter 2010).
3. For example, during Charles the Second's seventeenth-century reign, a Liverpool man said of the effect on his tenant: 'I was glad to send her to the house of correction since when she hath been much better' (Moore 1899: 33 cited by Sharpe 1984: 180).

4. Lodge (1974, 11) has characterised the establishment of the Home Office Research Unit, as a component of the 'inevitable…development in Great Britain of scientific criminological research' which has happened as a result of 'forces that for many years had been building up'. By way of illustration he refers to the establishment in 1931 of the Association for the Scientific Treatment of Criminals (later to become the Institute for the Study and Treatment of Delinquency) following work done by the Medical Research Council, and, in the same decade, correspondence between the penal reform campaigner Margery Fry and the Home Office on the need to start criminological research (13).
5. The National Crime Survey surveys were, according to Sparks (1981, 6) 'designed and implemented with what can only be described as indecent haste ... little more than two years was allowed for pretesting a new (and very expensive) research technique, in order to overcome the problems concerning the "reliability and accuracy" of survey findings which the President's Commission had uncovered. Even the little time that was allowed for pretesting was badly used.' Piloting efforts were 'puny and inept' and answered none of the questions which had been raised by the earlier surveys.

References

Bauman, Z. 1987. *Legislators and Interpreters*. Cambridge: Polity.

Beattie, J. 1986. *Crime and the Courts in England 1660–1800*. Oxford: Clarendon.

Bell, Emma. 2011. *Criminal Justice and Neoliberalism*. Houndmills: Palgrave Macmillan.

Bottoms, Anthony. 1995. The Philosophy and Politics of Punishment and Sentencing. In *The Politics of Sentencing Reform*, ed. Chris Clarkson and Rod Morgan, 17–49. Oxford: Clarendon.

Butler, Lord. 1974. The Foundation of the Institute of Criminology in Cambridge. In *Crime, Criminology and Public Policy*, ed. R. Hood, 1–10. London: Heineman.

Emsley, C. 1987. *Crime and Society in England 1750–1900*. Harlow: Longman.

Fielding, Nigel, and Martin Innes. 2006. Reassurance Policing, Community Policing and Measuring Police Performance. *Policing and Society* 16 (2): 127–145.

Foucault, M. 1972. *The Archaeology of Knowledge*. Trans. A.M. Sheridan Smith. London: Tavistock.

———. 1977. *Discipline and Punish: The Birth of the Prison*. London: Allen Lane.

———. 1991. Governmentality. In *The Foucault Effect: Studies in Governmentality*, ed. G. Burchell, C. Gordon, and P. Miller, 87–104. Chicago: Chicago University Press.

Garland, D. 1990. *Punishment and Modern Society*. Oxford: Oxford University Press.

———. 1996. The Limits of the Sovereign State: Strategies of Crime Control in Contemporary Society. *The British Journal of Criminology* 36 (4): 445–471.
Garland, D., and R. Sparks. 2000. Criminology, Social Theory and the Challenge of Our Times. In *Criminology and Social Theory*, ed. D. Garland and R. Sparks, 1–22. Oxford: Oxford University Press.
Garofalo, J. 1977. *Public Opinion About Crime: The Attitudes of Victims and Nonvictims in Selected Cities*. Albany: US Department of Justice.
Giddens, A. 1990. *The Consequences of Modernity*. Cambridge: Polity Press.
Hacking, I. 1991. How Should We Do the History of Statistics? In *The Foucault Effect: Studies in Governmentality*, ed. G. Burchell, C. Gordon, and P. Miller, 181–196. Chicago: University of Chicago Press.
Hanway, J. 1775. *The Defects of Police, the Cause of Immorality and the Continual Robberies Committed, Particularly in the Metropolis*. London: J Dodsley.
Hill, C. 1972. *The World Turned Upside Down: Radical Ideas During the English Revolution*. London: Temple Smith.
Hindelang, M.J. 1974. Public Opinion Regarding Crime, Criminal Justice and Related Topics. *Journal of Research in Crime and Delinquency* 11 (2): 101–116.
Hood, C. 1991. A Public Management for All Seasons? *Public Administration* 69: 3–19.
Hopkins-Burke, R. 2009. *An Introduction to Criminological Theory*. Cullompton: Willan.
Hough, Mike. 2003. Modernization and Public Opinion: Some Criminal Justice Paradoxes. *Contemporary Politics* 9 (2): 143–155.
Hough, Mike, and Patricia Mayhew. 1983. *The British Crime Survey: First Report*. London: Her Majesty's Stationary Office.
Hunter, J. 2010. *The Making of the Crofting Community*. Edinburgh: Birlinn.
Jones, T., B. MacLean, and J. Young. 1986. *The Islington Crime Survey*. Aldershot: Gower.
Kendall, G., and G. Whickham. 1999. *Using Foucault's Methods*. London: Sage.
Lee, Murray. 2007. *Inventing Fear of Crime: Criminology and the Politics of Anxiety*. Cullompton: Willan.
Lodge, T.S. 1974. The Founding of the Home Office Research Unit. In *Crime, Criminology and Public Policy*, ed. R. Hood, 11–24. London: Heinemann.
Moore, Sir. E. 1899. *Liverpool in King Charles the Second's Time*. Liverpool: Henry Young and Sons.
O'Farrell, Clare. 2005. *Michel Foucault*. London: Sage.
O'Malley, P. 1999. Volatile and Contradictory Punishment. *Theoretical Criminology* 3 (2): 175–196.
Ormrod, The Hon. Sir Roger. 1964. The Developing Relations Between the Law and the Social Sciences. *British Journal of Criminology* 4 (4): 320–331.
Pasquino, P. 1991. Criminology: The Birth of a Special Knowledge. In *The Foucault Effect: Studies in Governmentality*, ed. G. Burchell, C. Gordon, and P. Miller, 235–250. Hemel Hempstead: Harvester Wheatsheaf.

Pratt, J. 2002. *Punishment and Civilization: Penal Tolerance and Intolerance in Modern Society*. London: Sage.
Prebble, J. 1969. *The Highland Clearances*. London: Penguin Books.
Price, V., and P. Neijens. 1997. Opinion Quality in Public Opinion Research. *International Journal of Public Opinion Research* 9 (4): 336–360.
Reiner, R. 2010. *The Politics of the Police*. Oxford: Oxford University Press.
Rose, N. 1993. Government, Authority and Expertise in Advanced Liberalism. *Economy and Society* 22 (3): 283–300.
Salgado, G. 1977. *The Elizabethan Underworld*. Stroud: Sutton.
Sharpe, J.A. 1984. *Crime in Early Modern England 1550–1750*. Harlow: Longman.
Smart, B. 2002. *Michel Foucault*. London: Routledge.
Sparks, R.F. 1981. Surveys of Victimization – An Optimistic Assessment. In *Crime and Justice: An Annual Review of Research*, ed. M. Tonry and N. Morris, 1–60. Chicago: University of Chicago Press.
Squires, P. 1997. *Criminology and the "Community Safety" Paradigm: Safety, Power and Success and the Limits of the Local*. Belfast: British Criminology Conference Queens University.
Thompson, E.P. 1980. *The Making of the English Working Class*. Harmondsworth: Penguin.
Tonry, M., and D. Green. 2003. Criminology and Public Policy in the USA and UK. In *The Criminological Foundations of Penal Policy*, ed. L. Ashworth and A. Zedner. Oxford: Oxford University Press.
White, R., and F. Haines. 2008. *Crime and Criminology*. Melbourne: Oxford University Press.
Young, J. 1988. Radical Criminology in Britain: The Emergence of a Competing Paradigm. In *A History of British Criminology*, ed. P. Rock, 159–183. Oxford: Oxford University Press.
———. 1997. Left Realist Criminology: Radical in its Analysis, Realist in its Policy. In *The Oxford Handbook of Criminology*, ed. M. Maguire, R. Morgan, and R. Reiner. Oxford: Oxford University Press.
Young, J., and R. Matthews. 2003. New Labour, Crime Control and Social Exclusion. In *The New Politics of Crime and Punishment*, ed. R. Matthews and J. Young, 1–32. Cullompton: Willan.

CHAPTER 5

Genealogy: How the Public Confidence Agenda Got Its 'Hooks' into Criminal Justice

Abstract Turner argues that the social and political context from the late 1970s onwards allowed 'public confidence' to 'hook' into criminal justice discourse. The events and issues described are: (1) revelations about police misconduct and tense police-community relationships; (2) political debates about how to alleviate overcrowding in prisons taking place against the backdrop of Thatcherite authoritarian populism; (3) miscarriages of justice exposed during the late 1980s; (4) intense political contest between the ailing Conservative government and a resurgent Labour opposition during the 1990s; and (5) the debate about sentencing and minimum tariffs for murderers. The idea of public confidence was frequently invoked by groups *competing for power and influence* within the criminal justice arena, and the researchers themselves, responding to the increased opportunity to disseminate knowledge in this area, were not disinterested participants in the struggle for power and influence.

Keywords Public confidence in criminal justice • Foucault • Genealogy • Discourse analysis • Politics of criminal justice • Penal populism • New Labour • Miscarriages of justice • James Bulger • Myra Hindley • Michael Howard • Tony Blair

E.R. Turner, *Public Confidence in Criminal Justice*,
Critical Criminological Perspectives,
https://doi.org/10.1007/978-3-319-67897-9_5

> Must not power without public confidence be as precariously held as existence must be without a certainty of means? ('Query', *The London Chronicle*, Tuesday, 16 October to Thursday, 18 October 1764, Vol. XVI Issue. 1221 p. 371)

In this chapter I argue that the social and political context, as well as certain specific events from the late 1970s onwards, created an opening for the idea of public confidence to 'hook in' to criminal justice discourse, and also for a particular conceptualisation of confidence to dominate. By tracing the historical and political contingencies at work in this process, I unfold the core narrative of the story promised in my introduction to this book. It is a story that challenges the implication that the dominant survey-based aggregative, general, atomised, passive (AGAP) approach to researching public confidence applies value-free scientific reasoning to arrive at the most accurate method for researching an objective, pre-existing phenomenon. Instead I argue that the dominant approach to public confidence research was shaped by specific events, issues, and political struggles which created opportunities for a particular form of knowledge production to gain influence. Examining these events and issues helps us to understand the shifting political tides upon which the confidence research agenda floats.

The events and issues described are: (1) revelations about police misconduct during the 1950s and 1960s and tense police-community relationships in the 1970s and 1980s; (2) political debates about how to alleviate overcrowding in prisons taking place against the backdrop of the authoritarian populism of the Thatcher government (which fuelled concern amongst penal modernists about the government's failure to curb increasing punitiveness in rhetoric and policy); (3) miscarriages of justice exposed during the late 1980s leading to the Royal Commission which shaped penal discourse around the time of the appointment of the new Lord Chief Justice, Lord Taylor, in 1992; (4) some high-profile crime stories which unfolded in the early 1990s against a backdrop of intense political contest between the ailing Conservative government and a resurgent Labour opposition; and (5) the mid-1990s debate about sentencing and minimum tariffs for murderers.

I suggest that these conditions each contributed to public confidence 'hooking in' to discourses of crime and justice, as well as having helped to shape the dominant discourse of public confidence. The point which I want to illustrate here is that the idea of public confidence in the criminal justice system was frequently invoked by groups *competing for power and influence* within the criminal justice arena, and that the researchers themselves, who responded to the increased opportunity to disseminate knowledge in this area, were not disinterested participants in the struggle for power and influence.

5.1 Note on Method: Tracing the Movement of a Concept Through Texts

This chapter presents the second part of my genealogical analysis of the story of public confidence in the criminal justice system. It explores how, over a period of some 40 years, the idea of public confidence in the criminal justice system was able to '"hook" into normative ideas and commonsense notions' (Carrabine 2001, 269) within discourses on crime and criminal justice in England and Wales. I approach this task through an analysis of the publicly available records of the utterances of politicians and people working in the criminal justice field as reported in media discourses, and in the contents of parliamentary debates, policy documents, commissioned inquiries, and research reports. My focus is on when, where, and how the idea of public confidence entered into the discourse, including the material events and conditions against which it was deployed. I also trace the intertextual relationships at work, not just between the newspaper articles, but also between the newspaper articles and other textual genres, including political statements and debates and the content of policy and research documents.[1] By examining how texts relate to events (see Fairclough 2003, 37), it is possible to start

> to identify the details and accidents that accompany beginnings, the small deviations, the errors, the complete reversals, "the false appraisals and faulty calculations" that produced things, knowledges, and "truths" that continue to have value in contemporary settings. (Lee 2007, 10)

5.2 A Few 'Black Sheep': Police Misconduct and Public Confidence in Policing

The idea of public confidence first began to be regularly invoked in relation to the criminal justice arena with respect to policing. The Home Secretary's Christmas message to police officers in 1928 stressed the need for mutual confidence between the police and the public: '[t]he organization of the police and their relations with the public in this country are such that police work can be carried on with full efficiency only in an atmosphere of mutual confidence' (quoted in the *Times*, Friday, 07 December 1928). The idea that the police must retain the 'confidence' of the public to ensure that they can operate effectively is compatible with the historical usage of the term 'public confidence' which implicitly positions confidence as a prerequisite for the success of the object (be that a product, person, action, or organisation) to which confidence attaches. Invoking confidence also reflects and reinforces the orthodox (or 'cop-sided') understanding of British policing as 'policing by consent', a rather ambiguous and idealistic notion which nonetheless forms a continuing part of the professional self-identity of the British police (Reiner 2010, 44, 69).

There was a quantitative increase in media coverage of 'public confidence' in relation to policing from the mid-1950s onwards. This is not surprising, for as Reiner (2010, 78) has observed: 'After 1959 policing became a babble of scandalous revelation, controversy, and competing agendas for reform' threatening the fragile contract between police and public. By the 1950s Reiner suggests that there was majority acceptance of the position and legitimacy of the professionalised police force amongst those members of the public who were not routinely subjected to its coercive attentions (Reiner 2010, 77). The 1960s saw changes regarded as having eaten into the goodwill which the police had built up, including increases in the autonomy of chief constables and changes in police tactics which placed increasing emphasis on crime fighting through 'technology, specialization and managerial professionalism' and shifted more officers into motorised response roles, thus removing them from routine public contact (Reiner 2010, 79).

Perhaps just as damaging as the extraction of the police from a more community-based way of operating were a series of scandals involving misconduct and criminality perpetrated by police officers. It is in this context that the issue of public confidence in the police first starts to be discussed in the media. In a 1958 letter to the *Times*, referring to revelations of wrongdoing by the police, the Conservative MP William Shepherd observed that 'Recent events involving police in a number of areas have shaken public confidence' (*The Times*, Wednesday, 26 March 1958). In 1960, the Association of Chief Police Officers (ACPO) conference was headlined thus: 'Police Chiefs In Conference. Vital Need Of Public Confidence', and the coverage suggested that senior police officers saw their service as being under a cloud (*The Times*, Wednesday, 25 May 1960). Subsequent years yielded a recurring theme of stories of police abusing their positions for their own personal gain. For example: 'Three PCs sent to Prison. "Public confidence is shaken" court told' was how the *Times*, reported the imprisonment of three Welsh police officers for a series of offences (Tuesday, 21 March 1961). The following year, four police officers from Birmingham City Police were jailed for carrying out a string of offences whilst on night shift, raising the 'fear of a loss of public confidence' in the force (*The Times* Friday, 01 June 1962).

The prominence of these occurrences was such that the Royal Commission on Policing[2], appointed in 1960, and leading to the 1964 Police Act, was explicitly linked to the perceived need to restore public confidence in the police. However, neither the Commission nor the Act appeared to stem the steady flow of cases of police corruption, misconduct, and brutality which, if anything, became more prominent amidst the highly charged political atmosphere of the 1970s and 1980s.

From the 1970s onwards, reference to public confidence in the police was most frequently made in the context of a long-running debate about the need for reforms in the way in which complaints against the police were handled. In an early move in this debate, then Home Secretary Robert Carr talked of the need for complaints against the police to be independently reviewed so that the few 'black sheep' could be identified and 'public confidence' in policing restored (*The Times*, Saturday, 11 August 1973). The following year, Lord Scarman's (1975) report into the Red Lion Square Disorders of 15 June 1974, called for a police complaints procedure which would command 'public confidence' (reported in the *Times*, Friday, 28 February 1975). In the 1980s, police practice came under increasing scrutiny in relation to urban riots, including the 1981 disturbances in Brixton and on Merseyside. Lord Scarman was again requested to comment. He found that the breakdown in the relationship between the police and the community, and the community's loss of confidence in the police, had contributed to the riot (Scarman 1981).

Confidence in the police was first said to have been undermined by the behaviour of a minority of officers who had abused their position for personal gain. Later the focus shifted to the way the police more generally were discharging their professional duties, as concerns were raised about the policing of urban (particularly ethnic minority) communities, and disturbances within those communities, and also about dubious practices in securing evidence to support a conviction. In the criminal justice arena, then, the problem of 'public confidence' initially surfaced in relation to the relationship between the police and the public. Public confidence was regarded as an essential ingredient in legitimate and effective policing which was threatened, initially by the conduct of a few 'bad apples', and later by failures of police tactics within altered social environments. In this context, the value of confidence was self-evidently instrumental. The enemies of confidence were the reprehensible conduct of untrustworthy individuals, and, later, inappropriate methods of policing which were insufficiently checked by legal safeguards. However, although the idea of 'public confidence' was initially linked mainly to policing issues, during the early 1980s it came to be attached to a broader range of criminal justice activities.

5.3 'Vital to Maintain Public Confidence in the Criminal Justice System': Playing the Confidence Card

When the police were under pressure due to revelations about officer corruption, as well as facing questions about their ability to act as any kind of check on rising crime, and when Royal Commissions were deliberating changes in policy and procedure which could have profound implications for policing, neither senior officers nor their subordinates simply sat back and took the criticism. The Police Federation became increasingly politicised during this period (Reiner 2010, 89–91), and the late 1970s and early 1980s saw several senior police officers publicly hitting back at what they felt were unjustified attacks on the police that, they said, would prove damaging to public confidence. In their public pronouncements and protestations, police figures were often attempting to make a case for retaining their cherished political independence, resisting any further limitations on chief constables, or any moves to make the procedures for dealing with complaints against the police more transparent and independent.

Perhaps the most important, and certainly the most high-profile, police appointment of the 1970s was Robert Mark's tenure as Commissioner of the Metropolitan Police. Mark was not afraid to speak out on controversial topics and, in the most high-profile policing position in England, his statements usually received significant media coverage. His pronouncements often enraged professionals working in other parts of the criminal justice system. In 1975, he was criticised in the *New Law Journal* as having made statements which were 'clearly intended to undermine public confidence in the administration of justice' (*The Times*, Thursday, 21 August 1975).

Mark was not alone amongst senior police officers in making controversial and alarming public pronouncements. Merseyside Chief Constable Kenneth Oxford was quoted in the *Times* predicting the end of a way of life: 'If we cannot prevent the dreadful increase in crime, or at least contain it, the freedom and way of life we have been accustomed to enjoy for so long will vanish' (26 April 1978), whilst in the same paper his counterpart in Greater Manchester (James Anderton) conjured the image of a society literally saturated with crime: 'Crime soaks into society like water into a sponge', and the following year called for criminals to carry out forced labour in an article headlined 'Make thugs sweat in labour camps' (*The Daily Telegraph*, 15 June 1979). These headline-grabbing interventions from senior police officers seem unlikely to have assuaged public anxiety about rising crime, or contributed to a measured debate about penal affairs, and they prompted frustrated responses from professionals working directly with offenders. For example, in 1976, Christopher Andrews, then General Secretary of the British Association of Social Workers accused police officers of making remarks directly intended to undermine confidence in social work professionals (*The Times*, Friday, 07 May 1976).

What we can see in the public exchange of words between senior figures from different parts of the criminal justice apparatus is the way in which public confidence was increasingly invoked as something which was self-evidently necessary, and which ought not to be wilfully damaged. Media coverage of 'law and order', crime, and criminal justice around the 1979 election also offers some examples of how different organisations were being forced to consider how to gain the support of the public. See for example:

> Probation officers must reassure and convince the courts and the public that they, no less than the hard-line so-called law and order lobby believed in the rule of law. (*The Daily Telegraph*, 21 May 1979, reporting a speech by the President of the Association of Probation Officers)

> We have to face the fact that if the courts and the public are to have confidence in non-custodial disposals, such as supervision for the more serious offenders, then they have to be convinced that community-based schemes offer a real hope for combating delinquency and are not merely an expedient for saving public money. (Leon Brittain, then Home Secretary quoted in the *Daily Telegraph*, Thursday, 12 July 1979)

> Public confidence in the administration of justice was in danger of being impaired unless sentences of the courts were seen to be effective, Mr Roger Rickard, president of the Justices' Clerks' Society said yesterday. (*The Times*, 17 May 1979)

These extracts illustrate that the idea of public confidence was no longer being invoked exclusively or primarily in relation to policing, but instead was something which should attach to the criminal justice system as a whole. The persons responsible for invoking the idea of public confidence in this way were politicians and senior practitioners working within the criminal justice system. Their words were subsequently transmitted to wider audiences through the media, including newspapers carrying direct quotations from the texts of commons debates and from speeches at public events.

The debate about how to alleviate prison overcrowding was a key criminal justice focal point in the early 1980s, and it is in connection with this topic that we see the idea of public confidence being most frequently invoked. The Conservative government were adamant that direct interference on their part to reduce the number of prisoners within the system by changing the criteria for parole eligibility would damage public confidence. Home Secretary William Whitelaw stated that public opinion favoured transparency in sentencing and that the public wanted offenders to serve their full term. If the public perceived that offenders were not doing this then their confidence in the criminal justice system would fall (e.g. see the *Times*, Friday, 26 March 1982). Crucially, Whitelaw stated that it was the Home Secretary's duty to ensure that the public had confidence in the criminal justice system, and, in pursuance of this, he cited the need to maintain judicial independence, rejecting the idea that sentencing decisions should take any account of the latest figures on the prison population.

Furthermore, in a 1982 House of Commons debate on law and order, Whitelaw argued that sentencing (apart from the setting of maximums) should remain the preserve of the politically independent judiciary and magistracy and that this was 'vital to maintain public confidence in the criminal justice system. It would be a bad day if that power were ever to pass to politicians' (HC Debate, 25 March 1982, col. 1121). Whitelaw also made this point in a talk to the National Association of Prison Visitors, acknowledging challenging conditions in prisons but rejecting the idea of reducing the prison population at a time of rising crime, as this would 'undermine public confidence in the criminal justice system' (*The Times*, 13 May 1982). This is the first occasion on which the specific phrase public confidence in the criminal justice system appears in the media (although it was first used in the House of Commons by Ivan Lawrence MP in 1981, in a debate about the introduction of the Crown Prosecution Service (HC Debate, 20 November 1981, col. 576)).

The following year the new Home Secretary Leon Brittain stated that 'public confidence in the criminal justice system required sentences that reflect "society's deep abhorrence of violent crime"' (*The Times*, Wednesday, 12 October 1983).[3] Brittain also directly linked public confidence to the effectiveness of the police and criminal justice system. Announcing the establishment of the Crown Prosecution Service, he described it as a development which was an important step to 'increase public confidence, in the criminal justice system' (*The Times*, Saturday, 17 November 1984). The idea that public confidence requires sentences that reflect 'society's deep abhorrence of violent crime' was reprised in 1985 at Prime Minister's question time by Margaret Thatcher (reported in the *Times*, 15 March 1985). In an article in the *Guardian* later in the same year, the government's Chief Inspector of Prisons was quoted as saying that non-violent criminals should be given shorter sentences to alleviate prison overcrowding, adding that this would *not* damage public confidence in the criminal justice system (*The Guardian*, 25 October 1985).

In these examples, we see how the idea of public confidence started to be utilised by politicians and others in defence of a range of policy positions. Whatever the issue under discussion, public confidence could be invoked as the arbiter of what was, and was not, acceptable penal policy. It appeared almost as a trump card to be played as a way of negating the arguments put by those who expressed views which were in opposition to whatever it was that the government was planning to do or not do, or was already doing or not doing.

5.4 'This Sorry Chapter in the History of English Justice': The Royal Commission on Criminal Justice and Lord Taylor's Pledge

The late 1980s and early 1990s saw the emergence of new revelations about police fabrication of evidence and use of violence to extract confessions, most famously in the cases of the Guildford Four, Birmingham Six, and Maguire Seven. These revelations offered new opportunities for the idea of public confidence in the criminal justice system to have a prominent presence in political and media discourse. For example:

> The quashing of the Guildford bombing convictions is not just an ordinary kind of scandal. Public unease goes far beyond the question of possible wrongdoing by the Surrey police. The case has undermined public confidence in the criminal justice system itself. (*The Guardian*, 17 November 1989)

A Royal Commission on Criminal Justice was announced by the Home Secretary Kenneth Baker on the day that the Birmingham Six convictions were quashed (14 March 1991). In a speech (subsequently quoted in the *Times*, the *Guardian*, and the *Independent*), Baker said:

> The case, together with others which have occurred, raises a number of serious issues which must be a cause of concern to us all. It is of fundamental importance that the arrangements for criminal justice should secure the speedy conviction of the guilty and the acquittal of the innocent. When that is not achieved, public confidence is undermined. (HC Debates, 14 March 1991, col. 1109)

Baker was not the only politician to invoke the idea of public confidence, as reported by the *Independent*:

> A sharp response to the Court of Appeal decision came from Menzies Campbell QC, the Liberal Democrats' legal affairs spokesman, who called for a full judicial inquiry into "this sorry chapter in the history of English justice ... This grave miscarriage of justice has shaken public confidence in the judicial system and in particular in the role of the Court of Appeal. The Court of Appeal should have a wider investigative role than it now has in cases where there are serious doubts about the evidence which has been brought before a jury," Mr Campbell said outside the chamber. (*The Independent*, Friday, 15 March 1991)

In the aftermath of the Birmingham Six verdict, MPs launched a cross-party campaign to have the Lord Chief Justice, Lord Lane (who had presided over and rejected an earlier appeal by the Six), removed from his post by the Queen. At the time, the campaign was unsuccessful as, in the face of considerable media criticism, the legal establishment closed ranks around Lord Lane, and he received the backing of the Home Secretary and Prime Minister. However, less than a year later he vacated the post, a full year before his age would have meant he was required to retire. Lord Lane was replaced by Lord Taylor, who claimed that restoring public confidence in the criminal justice system was his mission in his new role, and who, for the rest of his life, would be cast in this light in subsequent media discourse. For example:

> Lord Justice Taylor, aged 61, takes over as the most senior judge at a time when, as he acknowledges, he has the task, with the rest of the legal profession, of restoring public confidence in the criminal justice system. (*The Times*, 26 February 1992)

> SIR Peter Taylor will be sworn in as Lord Chief Justice today with a pledge to restore public confidence in the criminal justice system in the wake of a series of miscarriages of justice. (*The Guardian*, 27 April 1992)

> Peter Taylor was appointed Lord Chief Justice in 1992 to restore public confidence in the criminal justice system, badly dented by a series of high profile miscarriages of justice. ('Obituary', *The Guardian*, 30 April 1997)

During the two years from the announcement of the Royal Commission until it reported, public confidence in the criminal justice system was overwhelmingly referred to in the context of discussions of miscarriages of justice. Senior figures within the criminal justice system used the term in this sense, for example:

> I and my staff are acutely aware of the effect which miscarriages of justice have on the public confidence in the criminal justice system. However, it is my duty to make the right decision, not the expedient one. (Open letter from Barbara Mills QC, the Director of Public Prosecutions, defending her decision not to prosecute any of the police officers involved in the wrongful conviction of Stefan Kiszko. Published in the *Guardian*, 22 May 1992)

> The perceived decline of public confidence in the criminal justice system is another issue of concern. Highly publicised cases of miscarriage of justice undermine the improvements that have now been made to the integrity of our evidence gathering process. (From the annual report by the Metropolitan Police Commissioner Sir Peter Imbert, quoted in the *Guardian*, 30 July 1992)

From 1991 until 1993, then, discourses of public confidence in criminal justice focused on the adequacy of the procedures used to gather evidence and secure convictions and the trust invested in the professionals responsible for ensuring that the procedures were followed. Discourses of public confidence were not, at this time, invoked in relation to issues of prison overcrowding and sentencing.

5.5 Criminal Justice Politics Get 'Tough'

During the early years of the 1990s, then, the idea of public confidence in the criminal justice system was almost entirely invoked in relation to the issue of miscarriages of justice, the associated Royal Commission on Criminal Justice, and the appointment of the new Lord Chief Justice, Lord Taylor. However, by July 1993, the month when the Royal Commission's findings were due to be released, the political and social landscape had changed dramatically and the public confidence discourse had shifted. At this time, the Conservative government appeared increasingly weak in the face of a resurgent Labour party, and events which unfolded in the first half of 1993 only increased the pressure on the government in this regard.

The killing of toddler James Bulger by two ten-year-old boys in February 1993 prompted national shock and outrage. The then Shadow Home Secretary, Tony Blair, reacted in a way which raised his own profile and aligned the Labour party with a new slogan: 'tough on crime, tough on the causes of crime'. In the aftermath of the Bulger case, and for the first time since polling began, Labour were regarded by more people than the Conservatives as having the 'best policies for dealing with crime' (ICM/*The Guardian* Poll, March 1993). The Bulger case is often cited as a watershed moment in debates about crime and justice in England and Wales (e.g. see Green 2008). It certainly seems to have coincided with the moment at which Labour over took the Conservatives in the polls on crime and justice issues, and political rhetoric around crime and justice became substantially more hard line. However, there were other events in 1993 which may have been just as significant in reshaping the political landscape, and shifting the discourse on public confidence.

In June 1993, two men from a small village in Norfolk were jailed for five years in relation to events which had occurred on 12 January that year. The two men admitted kidnapping and threatening a local youth who they believed to be responsible for a spate of local burglaries. They were said to have acted when it became apparent that the police and criminal justice system were either unable or unwilling to take action to bring the perpetrators of the crimes to justice. Media coverage of the case throughout June linked it to a more general theme of a criminal justice system struggling to cope due to a combination of inadequate resources and unduly constrictive legislation. Headlines like 'A Village Cheated of Justice' (*Daily Mail*, 17 June 1993) and 'Middle England hits back' (*The Sunday Times*, 20 June 1993) indicate the angle taken by the media, which linked the case into a much broader discourse about a crisis in criminal justice, for example:

> THE five-year jail term handed down to the two Norfolk vigilantes was more than a rogue judge being a bit heavy-handed. It was more even than a tough judicial warning against people taking the law into their own hands. It was a desperate and no doubt instinctive attempt by the judge to hold together a system of justice that has now catastrophically cracked open. Yet it has merely exacerbated the crisis. (*The Observer*, 20 June 1993)

In the same month, the papers reported the case of Joseph Elliott, who, whilst 'high on drink and drugs', caused criminal damage to his neighbour's car and, when confronted by his neighbour, stabbed and killed him. Elliott was acquitted by the jury on the basis that he had acted in self-defence. Conservative MPs and police officers railed against the decision, demanding changes in the law. The headline in the *Guardian* in July read 'Vigilante's stabbing prompts self-defence study; Conservative MPs demand changes in the law to "restore public confidence in the criminal justice system"'. This was the first occasion on which the phrase 'public confidence in the criminal justice system' was used in a newspaper headline. The article reported that

> the Home Secretary is to review the way the law of self-defence works following the acquittal of a man who admitted stabbing his neighbour to death. Michael Howard faced demands from Conservative MPs for law changes designed, they said, to restore public confidence in the power of the criminal justice system to convict the guilty as well as acquit the innocent. (*The Guardian*, 15 July 1993)

In this article, the idea of public confidence in the criminal justice system has drifted loose of the issue of miscarriages of justice where innocent people have been jailed, and is instead applied to an apparent failure of natural justice, where a man apparently attempting to protect his property has been killed and the law is unable to convict his killer of murder.

So, at a time of increasing political tension, with the two main political parties locked in a battle to be seen as *the* party of 'law and order', the idea of public confidence became attached to a new kind of problem with criminal justice. It stopped being invoked in relation to issues of police misconduct and miscarriages of justice and, instead, began to be used in relation to the problem of criminals 'getting away with it' and law-abiding members of the public feeling unable to rely on the criminal justice system to protect them.

As a result, as the *Times* legal correspondent Frances Gibb noted at the time, the report of the Royal Commission which had started work in 1991 would, in 1993, be delivered into a vastly altered political climate from that in which it had begun its work: 'public opinion on law and order, as one government minister put it, has "turned a cartwheel" and concern about the rights of the defendant in the criminal justice process is increasingly eclipsed by calls for tougher action on criminals' (*The Times*, 18 May 1993). The day before the Royal Commission was due to release its findings, the *Times* covered research by the *Solicitors Journal*, which suggested:

> Most people have lost faith in the system of British justice as the best in the world and want an independent tribunal to investigate miscarriages of justice, according to a survey today. The Solicitors Journal survey of 1,000 people in England and Wales found that only 21 per cent agreed that the British system of justice was the best in the world. Some 45 per cent disagreed. There was also a big loss of confidence in the ability of the police to catch criminals compared with a decade ago, the survey showed, with backing for more officers on the streets. (*The Times*, 5 July 1993)

By the time the findings of the Royal Commission on Criminal Justice were published on 6 July, they appeared hopelessly out of step with the political zeitgeist. On the Sunday following the publication of the findings, the *Observer* carried a substantial article devoted to presenting a police perspective on the recommendations:

> To Britain's busiest murder squad, last week's Royal Commission report on criminal justice was a failure, taking the country closer to the 'doomsday scenario' in which the public, dismayed by the workings of the courts, loses faith in the rule of law. ... "You are getting people returned to the streets who have committed very serious offences, and the criminal law has no sanction against them. Ultimately, there will be a backlash," says Detective Chief Superintendent Tom Williamson, who runs east London's Area Major

> Investigation Pool (Amip). The commission, he says, "tinkers round the edges of the adversarial system without recommending genuine, radical reform. Meanwhile, public confidence in the criminal justice system is draining away." (*The Observer*, 11 July 1993)

This article is a striking example of how the changed social and political environment enabled the police to regain some control of the confidence discourse and redirect its focus away from the potential misconduct of their own organisation and onto the workings of the courts.

In August 1993, Tony Blair increased the pressure on the weak Conservative government, seizing on polling evidence about the public's lack of 'confidence' in various criminal justice functions. The Home Secretary Michael Howard responded by claiming that Labour were 'soft on crime' (*The Guardian*, 31 Aug 1993). In September, the papers reported that Michael Howard was holding a 'two day summit on how to restore public confidence in the criminal justice system'. In October, the *Guardian* reported that the government would give law and order 'top billing' at their annual conference:

> the shattered public confidence in the criminal justice system is reflected in the 244 resolutions tabled by constituency parties demanding action. Mr Major is expected to devote a third of his conference speech on Friday to the issue. ... In an attempt to rescue the position, Mr Howard will ignore the recommendations of the two-year Royal Commission on Criminal Justice'. (*The Guardian*, 2 October 1993)

In Howard's now-infamous speech to the conference he argued:

> Prison works. It ensures that we are protected from murderers, muggers and rapists - and it makes many who are tempted to commit crime think twice ... This may mean that more people will go to prison. I do not flinch from that. We shall no longer judge the success of our system of justice by a fall in our prison population.

Forced to defend his claims against criticisms from the judiciary, the *Times* reported that Howard accused them of 'misunderstanding his speech ... and declared that putting offenders in prison prevented fresh crime and protected victims. Taking away public confidence in the criminal justice system might be an invitation to the vigilante he said' (*The Times*, 18 October 1993).

The idea of 'public confidence' in the criminal justice system featured prominently in media discourse throughout the rest of 1993 and into 1994 as the term became a favoured reference point in any discussion of criminal justice matters. For example:

> Mr Howard claimed that his "consistent strategy to fight crime" would restore public confidence in the criminal justice system. (*The Guardian*, 4 May 1994)

> Michael Howard is adamant that without the tough action he announced last year, public confidence in the criminal justice system would have collapsed. (*The Times*, 13 Oct 1994)

By this stage journalists had started to use the term 'public confidence' themselves, rather than quoting it directly from politicians or criminal justice officials. For example:

> The rate at which police forces caught criminals declined again last year, according to a The Guardian survey of detection rates across England and Wales. ... The findings were described last night by Tony Blair, the shadow home secretary, as devastating and will alarm Home Office ministers and senior police officers battling to restore public confidence in the criminal justice. (*The Guardian*, 31 January 1994)

The term 'public confidence' in the criminal justice system, then, proved to be both versatile and mobile. Having been applied to a range of criminal justice issues (including police misconduct, miscarriages of justice, prison overcrowding, sentencing of offenders, attempts to reintroduce the death penalty), it migrated from the terminology of pollsters and the speeches and comments of politicians and criminal justice officials, into debates in the House of Parliament, journalistic turns of phrase, policy documents, and even the summing up of cases by lawyers and members of the judiciary.

As the 1990s progressed, the practice of 'playing the confidence card' (described above) continued to be used. For example, the day after the publication of the Royal Commission's findings, the Bar Council chairman, John Rowe QC said the following:

> It is vital that there is public confidence in the criminal justice system, and we are therefore deeply concerned that one of the Commission's major rec-

ommendations is to abolish automatic right of defendants to trial by jury. (Quoted in the *Daily Mail*, 7 July 1993)

As the government appeared to stall on key recommendations from the Royal Commission on Criminal Justice, including establishing a body to review claimed miscarriages of justice, the Chair of the Bar Council once again intervened:

> It is important that the Government does not allow this important recommendation of the Royal Commission to wither on the vine. Public confidence in the criminal justice system will be endangered if this widely supported and important step is further delayed. (Quoted in the *Times*, 16 November 1994)

The Law Society also invoked public confidence to express their resistance to proposed abolition of the right to silence:

> The Law Society says that the Government has "failed to recognise the reasons why the Royal Commission on Criminal Justice was set up in 1991" namely lack of public confidence in the criminal justice system. "The main effect of this bill will be an even greater risk of miscarriages without increased convictions of the guilty." A clear majority of the Royal Commission said the right to silence should not be abolished. (*The Times*, 11 Jan 1994)

Meanwhile, when the idea of a free vote on the reintroduction of the death penalty was mooted, the Chief Constable of Humberside said capital punishment would 'only add to the lack of public confidence in the criminal justice system. I find capital punishment abhorrent and do not consider it to be a protection for police officers' (quoted in the *Guardian*, 21 February 1994).

However, despite these attempts to use public confidence to oppose measures considered to be detrimental to the rights of the accused, the use of the idea of 'public confidence' in a criminal justice context in reference to issues other than the inadequacies of the courts and the idea of offenders 'getting away with it' became increasingly rare in this period. It was in connection with the particular issue of sentencing, as well as with three notorious offenders, that the idea of public confidence in the criminal justice system was most regularly invoked in the latter part of the 1990s.

5.6 'A Child's Screams Must Not Be Stifled': Minimum Tariffs for Murder

A direct and explicit connection between the James Bulger case and the public confidence agenda did not emerge until a disagreement arose between the Home Secretary and the Judiciary about the minimum period which his killers should serve in custody before being considered eligible for release. The original tariff, set by the trial judge in November 1993, was that they should serve a minimum of eight years. In December 1993, the Lord Chief Justice increased this to ten years. In July 1994, Home Secretary Michael Howard decided that Thompson and Venables should serve a minimum of 15 years. Howard's decision, according to the Home Office press release, was based on 'the judicial recommendations as well as all other relevant factors including the circumstances of the case, public concern about the case and the need to maintain public confidence in the criminal justice system' (quoted in Green 2008, 2).

The Home Office press release on the matter was quoted verbatim or closely paraphrased across the media at the time, and echoed at every subsequent occasion upon which the matter was discussed. Thus, the idea that the Home Secretary must take 'public confidence in the criminal justice system' into account when setting minimum tariffs became a common place refrain at this time. The public confidence principle has no basis in legislation. Rather, it can be traced back to the judgment in a case from the 1980s, referred to by Lord Beaverbrook in a House of Lords debate from 1986:

> The final decision [on parole] rests with the Secretary of State. I can do no better than to quote the words of the noble and learned Lord, Lord Scarman, when giving judgment in the case of Findlay et al which was brought before the House of Lords: "Neither the Parole Board nor the judiciary can be as close or as sensitive to public opinion as a Minister responsible to Parliament and to the electorate. He has to judge the public acceptability of early release and to determine the policies needed to maintain public confidence in the system of criminal justice. This must be why Parliament saw as necessary the duality of the parole system: without the advice and recommendation of a body capable of assessing the risk of early release the Secretary of State was not to act; but, having received such advice and recommendation, he was to authorise early release only if he himself was satisfied that it was in the public interest that he should". It is against that background—above all, the need to pursue a policy in relation to parole

> which maintains public confidence in the criminal justice system—that my right honourable friend the Home Secretary is following the practice of his predecessor in exercising his discretion restrictively in cases involving the most serious offences of violence and drug trafficking. (Lord Beaverbrook, HL Debate, 4 November 1986, Col. 1088, emphasis added)

Howard's decision to extend the minimum tariff for Thompson and Venables and his subsequent overruling in 1996 by the Court of Appeal and House of Lords were early episodes in a long-running debate about who should set minimum tariffs in cases of murder, and on what basis. Interestingly, at the beginning of this long-running dispute between politicians and the judiciary, Lord Woolf stated that, by courting direct conflict with the judiciary, Howard himself had 'undermined public confidence in the criminal justice system' (*The Guardian*, 31 July 1996). The debate was only concluded when the Criminal Justice Act 2003 outlawed politicians' involvement in setting tariffs.

The debate over minimum tariffs and eligibility for consideration for parole also raged around the case of Myra Hindley, and inspired some particularly intemperate media coverage. For example, under the headline 'A child's screams must not be stifled by the do-gooders; The Case for Myra Hindley Never Being Released', Conservative MP David Mellor wrote:

> Any day now the Home Secretary has to announce a decision which, if he gets it wrong, will strike at the very heart of public confidence in the criminal justice system. The courts have insisted that every convicted murderer serving a life sentence should be told the minimum term he or she must serve. So Michael Howard is brought face to face with the issue Home Secretaries most dread - whether Britain's most hated woman, Myra Hindley, can ever be released. I hope his answer is No. I shouldn't care to be in his shoes if it isn't. (*The Mail*, Sunday, 10 July 1994)

Media coverage of Hindley's attempt to have her whole life tariff overturned during 1996 featured repeated references to the Home Secretary's responsibility to take account of the need to maintain public confidence in the criminal justice system.

The dispute about minimum tariffs was one aspect of a more general rift between the judiciary and politicians which opened up around the time of the Royal Commission reporting its ill-timed findings. The idea of public confidence in the criminal justice system featured often in the media coverage of some very heated exchanges over the issue of judicial independence and sentencing from the mid-1990s until Labour's 1997 general election victory. For example, when judges, including Lord Justice Taylor, attacked government proposals to introduce mandatory minimum sentences, a *Times* editorial leapt to the defence of the Home Secretary:

> The first duty of the Home Secretary is to maintain public confidence in the criminal justice system. It is self-evident that public confidence in sentencing policy has been eroded and that Parliament must soon address the problem. (*The Times*, 13 October 1995)

And, when the Bill to introduce mandatory minimums had its second reading in the House of Lords, the Home Office Minister Baroness Blatch was quoted as saying that it would 'provide protection and reassurance for the public, and thereby help to improve public confidence in the criminal justice system' (*The Times*, 2 January 1997).

5.7 Looking Back in Anger? Political and Media Discourse Meets Criminological Concern about 'Penal Populism'

Considering the political developments described in the previous two sections, it is unsurprising that the late twentieth and early twenty-first centuries saw criminologists and penal scholars analysing what most regarded as an unwelcome punitive shift in criminal justice policy in Anglophone jurisdictions (e.g. see Bell 2011; Freiberg 2001; Garland 2000, 2001; Hallsworth 2000; Loader 2011; Pratt 2007; Roberts et al. 2003; Ryan 1999; Wacquant 2009).[4] Proposed explanations varied, but it was generally accepted (and indeed is borne out above) that during the 1980s and 1990s debates about criminal justice became more politically prominent and heated as politicians appeared to feel increasingly pressured to appear responsive to the views of the public in this area of policy (Downes and Morgan 1997). Criminologists, as the 'experts' on what is effective in dealing with crime, felt that they had suffered a loss of status in the criminal justice policymaking process (e.g. see Brereton 1996; Garland 1996, 2000, 2001; Roberts et al. 2003; Young and Matthews 2003; Young 2003; Grimshaw 2004; Tonry 2004; Loader 2006, 2010).

One of the most widely cited accounts of the factors shaping penal policy is the 1995 paper by Anthony Bottoms (1995), in which he coined the term 'populist punitiveness'.

> Populist punitiveness occurs when politicians 'believe that the adoption of a "populist punitive" stance will satisfy a particular electoral constituency ... the term "populist punitiveness" is intended to convey the notion of politicians tapping into, and using for their own purposes, what they believe to be the public's generally punitive stance. (39–40)

Roberts et al. (2003) adapted Bottoms' term and described what they call 'penal populism', a political approach which, unconcerned with the wisdom of slavishly following public preferences, 'involves the exploitation of misinformed opinion in the pursuit of electoral advantage' (Roberts et al. 2003, 7).

Interestingly, Roberts et al. suggest that evidence of New Labour's populism can be seen in their concern with 'public confidence in the criminal justice system' and being seen to be 'tough' on crime (52–3). Similarly, Downes and Morgan (1997) suggested that Labour's talking 'tough' on law and order meant that by 1997 their party attracted greater 'public confidence' on this issue than the conservatives (129). Populism, then, was specifically linked to attempting to gain the 'confidence' of the public on the issue of law and order, with 'confidence' understood here as indicated through opinion poll ratings. It is claimed that Labour boosted their opinion poll ratings on the issue of crime during the 1990s by emphasising their 'tough' criminal justice credentials.

As noted in Chap. 2, research demonstrating that the public generally do not have an 'accurate' notion of either the volume and distribution of crime, or the nature of the state response, has been a staple of the criminological knowledge base since at least the 1980s. Seen against this light, the suggestion that 'public dissatisfaction [with the criminal justice system] stems from public ignorance of the system' (Hough and Roberts 1998, 27) appears rather like a defensive manoeuvre by criminologists deeply concerned about a punitive shift in policy leading to a downgrading of expertise in the policymaking process.

Concerns about penal populism, then, may well have incentivised some researchers to engage with empirical research on public attitudes (including public confidence), in a well-meaning attempt to regain control over the evidence base in this area, wresting it away from unreliable media polls and thus attempting to initiate a shift in the politicians' approach. However, as argued in Chap. 2, whilst showing themselves willing to challenge politicians' tendencies to be swayed by media representations of public opinion, few (if any) researchers working in this area have challenged the idea that public opinion has an independent existence prior to the application of a specific research mechanism which makes it visible and representable. Instead, researchers have simply sought to replace unreliable media polls with their own, more sophisticated, methods.

5.8 Conclusion

The early- to mid-1990s are often identified as a watershed period in penal politics in England and Wales. Events taking place during 1993, in particular the murder of James Bulger and Michael Howard's infamous claim that 'prison works', are often referred to as pivotal in establishing crime as a core election issue and consolidating the more punitive approach which underpinned the unprecedented rise in the prison population which followed. This chapter has highlighted the presence of the idea of 'public confidence in the criminal justice system' as a discursive backdrop to these fundamentally *political* shifts. It has also drawn attention to earlier uses of the idea, prior to the 1990s, to show that, over time, the use and issue-orientation of the concept has shifted.

This analysis demonstrates that the idea of 'public confidence' first 'hooked' into criminal justice discourse via reactions to emerging evidence about police corruption in the 1960s and 1970s. Then, once the idea became established in political and media discourse, it started to be deployed by competing interest groups doing what I have called 'playing the confidence card'. Claims to know what 'public confidence' in justice required, and when and why it was being undermined, were made by a series of prominent figures, from chief constables to representatives of the social work and legal professions. The claims were made to condemn or to justify particular positions, and thus to protect and preserve certain values and indeed shore up the political and/or professional power of different groups.

In the late 1980s and early 1990s revelations about police misconduct and associated miscarriages of justice, led to claims that the criminal justice system was facing a crisis of confidence. This prompted the appointment of a Royal Commission. However, before the commission had reported its findings, a number of high-profile and hugely symbolic criminal justice-related events (including incidents of vigilantism and the murder of James Bulger) had taken place against the backdrop of an intensification of political rhetoric around crime and justice. At this point the discourse of public confidence was rapidly turned on its head: away from the focus on miscarriages of justice and towards the idea of criminals 'getting away with it'.

During the period from 1993 to 1997, this new understanding of public confidence, as primarily linked to issues of sentencing and punishment, became 'hooked' into political and media discourse around criminal justice. This shift happened as crime and justice (or 'law and order') became an important political battleground in the build-up to the 1997 general election. The increasing determination of the Labour party to compete with the Conservatives on this issue marked a significant departure from the stance which they had taken on the issue in previous decades. Changes within the criminological field that occurred during the 1980s, in particular the emergence of the 'left realist' perspective discussed in the previous chapter, are likely to have played some part here (although not the part that left realists themselves may have wished for). However, it also seems likely that in seeking to provide their own representations of public opinion to the politicians, criminologists were seeking to reassert their position in relation to criminal justice policymaking, against a trend towards what they identified as 'penal populism'.

In the final and concluding chapter of this book, I bring together the different parts of the story I have told so far to critique the idea that a survey-based AGAP approach to public confidence allows disinterested researchers to provide objective representations of a pre-existing phenomenon. I then consider the 'costs to existence' imposed by the dominant approach to researching public confidence and make some suggestions as to how we might move towards alternatives.

Notes

1. For more information on the method used, see Appendix 2.
2. See Royal Commission on the Police (1962).
3. Although, in an indication of the Conservative government's bifurcated strategy, Brittain signalled that punitive sentencing for violent criminals required that less serious offenders be kept out of prison where possible.
4. Although as Bosworth (2011) points out, one can identify many examples of initiatives and innovations which buck this punitive trend.

References

1962. *Royal Commission on the Police: Final Report Cmnd 1728*. London: HMSO.

Bell, Emma. 2011. *Criminal Justice and Neoliberalism*. Houndmills: Palgrave Macmillan.

Bosworth, Mary. 2011. Penal Moderation in the United States? Yes We Can. *Criminology & Public Policy* 10 (2): 335–343.

Bottoms, Anthony. 1995. The Philosophy and Politics of Punishment and Sentencing. In *The Politics of Sentencing Reform*, ed. Chris Clarkson and Rod Morgan, 17–49. Oxford: Clarendon.

Brereton, David. 1996. Does Criminology Matter? Crime, Politics and the Policy Process. *Current Issues in Criminal Justice* 8 (1): 82–88.

Carrabine, J. 2001. Unmarried Motherhood 1830–1990: A Genealogical Analysis. In *Discourse as Data: A Guide for Analysis*, ed. M. Wetherall, S. Taylor, and S.J. Yates, 267–310. London: Sage.

Downes, David, and Rod Morgan. 1997. Dumping the "Hostages to Fortune"? The Politics of Law and Order in Post-War Britain. In *The Oxford Handbook of Criminology*, ed. M. Maguire, R. Morgan, and R. Reiner, 87–134. Oxford: Oxford University Press.

Fairclough, Nigel. 2003. *Analysing Discourse: Textual Analysis for Social Research*. London: Routledge.

Freiberg, Arie. 2001. Affective Versus Effective Justice: Instrumentalism and Emotionalism in Criminal Justice. *Punishment and Society* 3 (2): 265–278.

Garland, David. 1996. The Limits of the Sovereign State: Strategies of Crime Control in Contemporary Society. *The British Journal of Criminology* 36 (4): 445–471.

———. 2000. The Culture of High Crime Societies: Some Preconditions of Recent 'Law and Order' Policies. *British Journal of Criminology* 40 (2): 347–375.

———. 2001. *The Culture of Control*. Oxford: Oxford University Press.

Green, David A. 2008. *When Children Kill Children: Penal Populism and Political Culture*. Oxford: Oxford University Press.

Grimshaw, R. 2004. Whose Justice? Principal Drivers of Criminal Justice Policy, Their Implications for Stakeholders, and Some Foundations for Critical Policy Departures. Selected Papers from the 2004 British Criminology Conference, Portsmouth July 2004. Accessed 30/11/2009 at http://www.britsoccrim.org/v7.htm

Hallsworth, Simon. 2000. Rethinking the Punitive Turn: Economies of Excess and the Criminology of the Other. *Punishment and Society* 2 (2): 145–160.

Hough, Mike, and Julian V. Roberts. 1998. *Attitudes to Punishment: Findings from the British Crime Survey*. London: Home Office.

Lee, Murray. 2007. *Inventing Fear of Crime: Criminology and the Politics of Anxiety*. Cullompton: Willan.

Loader, I. 2006. Fall of the 'Platonic Guardians': Liberalism, Criminology and Political Responses to Crime in England and Wales. *British Journal of Criminology* 46: 561–586.

———. 2010. For Penal Moderation: Notes Towards a Public Philosophy of Punishment. *Theoretical Criminology* 14 (3): 349–367.

———. 2011. Playing with Fire? Democracy and the Emotions of Crime and Punishment. In *Emotions, Crime and Justice*, ed. Susanne Karstedt, Ian Loader, and Heather Strang, 347–362. Oxford: Hart.

Pratt, John. 2007. *Penal Populism*. Abingdon: Routledge.

Reiner, R. 2010. *The Politics of the Police*. Oxford: Oxford University Press.

Roberts, Julian V., Loretta J. Stalans, David Indermaur, and Mike Hough. 2003. *Penal Populism and Public Opinion: Lessons from Five Countries*. Oxford: Oxford University Press.

Ryan, Mick. 1999. Penal Policy Making Towards the Millenium: Elites and Populists; New Labour and the New Criminology. *International Journal of the Sociology of Law* 27 (1): 1–22.

Scarman, Lord. 1975. *The Red Lion Square Disorders of 15 June 1974, Cmd. 5919*. London: HMSO.

———. 1981. *The Brixton Disorders 10–12 April 1981*. London: HMSO.

Tonry, M. 2004. *Thinking About Crime: Sense and Sensibility in American Penal Culture*. Oxford: Oxford University Press.

Wacquant, Loic. 2009. *Prisons of Poverty*. Minneapolis: University of Minnesota Press.

Young, J. 2003. Winning the Fight Against Crime? New Labour, Populism and Lost Opportunities. In *The New Politics of Crime and Punishment*, ed. R. Matthews and J. Young, 33–47. Cullompton: Willan.

Young, J., and R. Matthews. 2003. New Labour, Crime Control and Social Exclusion. In *The New Politics of Crime and Punishment*, ed. R. Matthews and J. Young, 1–32. Cullompton: Willan.

CHAPTER 6

Conclusion: Researchers and the Making of Political Worlds

Abstract Bringing together the observations from the analysis provided in the previous four chapters, Turner argues that public confidence in criminal justice never was a pre-existing, independently 'real' phenomenon: it had to be constructed and was carved out of the raw materials of historical circumstance and political opportunity. This agenda has 'costs to existence': influenced by and contributing to a wider political culture that de-emphasises engagement and dialogue between the public and policy-makers and casts the public as passive ill-informed *individual* consumers reliant upon experts to inform them about 'reality' and to communicate their opinions to their elected representatives. In assembling a public, researchers create a picture of society which may be reflected back into that society. They are involved in the making of political worlds. As such, they should not hide behind an objectivist epistemology in order to avoid acknowledging the responsibilities they have as inevitably political actors.

Keywords Public confidence in criminal justice • The politics of research • Public opinion • Democracy • Democratic citizenship

As the introduction to this book indicated, I was motivated to write it because I feel that the dominant approach to researching public opinion about the criminal justice system (which focused on the idea of 'public

E.R. Turner, *Public Confidence in Criminal Justice*,
Critical Criminological Perspectives,
https://doi.org/10.1007/978-3-319-67897-9_6

confidence') can be bettered. Public confidence in criminal justice never was a pre-existing, independent, phenomenon—pure, real, awaiting, and deserving investigation—it had to be constructed as an object for research. As the preceding chapters have shown, the public confidence agenda was carved out of the raw materials of historical circumstance and political opportunity. In this concluding chapter, I consider in more depth the consequences of the public confidence agenda—its 'costs to existence' (Burchell 1996)—and reflect on ways to move beyond the current state of affairs.

6.1 Recap of the Argument so Far

In Chap. 2, I argued that, despite early criticisms of survey-based aggregative, general, atomised, passive (AGAP) approaches to public opinion, the steady accretion of published studies cast in this mould established a dominant discourse of 'public confidence in the criminal justice system' as a real, measurable thing, with identifiable causes. This conception of confidence was linked to an agenda for policy and practice organised around educating the public about 'the facts' of crime and criminal justice. I also pointed out that the empirical research tended to produce repetitive and rather uninteresting findings, and that it is possible to point to several episodes of mis- or over-interpretation of research findings which gave the knowledge base a more solid appearance than the available evidence warranted.

In Chap. 3, I identified the hierarchical 'grid of specification' implicit in the dominant discourse of public confidence; described the way in which confidence research 'violates' the phenomena which it purports to represent through certain 'procedures of intervention'; argued that the decision about how to do confidence research is a value-judgement about what kinds of objects to produce, make visible, and represent; and suggested that the dominance of survey research has been achieved based on a misrepresentation of this value-judgement as a scientific matter of choosing the most appropriate method. This misrepresentation has been used by some proponents of the survey-based approach to dismiss or undermine alternative approaches to understanding what the public think and feel (including deliberative approaches).

In Chap. 4, I argued that the 'problem' of public confidence in the criminal justice system could not exist unless the public had been progressively excluded from a professionalised system for dealing with criminal deviance, and had their accustomed ways of knowing about crime and justice not been increasingly discredited by new groups of 'experts', applying new 'modern' ways of knowing. Under these conditions, most members of the public no longer have direct personal access to the 'reality' of crime and punishment and thus must instead trust in the 'expert system' (Giddens 1990, 22) that assumes the role of accurately describing 'reality'. Furthermore, in democratic societies, the 'opinions' of members of the public must be seen to count for something when policies are made and, during the twentieth century, mechanisms were devised to measure those opinions, mechanisms that have been adopted by researchers to 'measure' public confidence (or so they claim). Thus, the idea of public confidence in criminal justice in its late twentieth-century incarnation was *always* about the 'gap' that arose in the modern era between 'expert' and 'lay' ways of knowing, and the problems this causes in and for democracies.

In Chap. 5, I showed that from the mid-twentieth century onwards the idea of 'public confidence in the criminal justice system' provided a discursive accompaniment to fundamentally *political* shifts, and that its meaning and significance changed over time. By the 1990s, when the term 'public confidence' became more securely 'hooked' in to media and political discourses around criminal justice, it was most frequently being deployed as a rhetorical device by individuals or groups seeking to gain advantage in a series of heated political debates, including in relation to the emotive issue of who should set the minimum sentence tariff for murder in high profile cases. Looking back at this era, some commentators on penal politics have argued that attempts by the main political parties to win the confidence of the public in relation to 'law and order' underpinned the politicisation of this area of policy. The involvement of some of these same commentators in the production of research on public confidence indicates that it was not only criminal justice professionals and politicians who got involved with what I have called 'playing the confidence card'. Claiming the right to know about the direction of public opinion, and the factors driving it, seems to have been important for many different groupings interested in influencing the shape of criminal justice policy.

Over the four analytical chapters I have shown that researchers making claims about 'public confidence in the criminal justice system' have frequently taken a highly topical and evocative 'lay concept' (Durkheim 1938, 37) and worked with that lay concept as if it referred unproblematically to some real, pre-existing object. The error, to repeat Durkheim's words, is this:

> We are so accustomed to use these terms, and they recur so constantly in our conversation, that it seems unnecessary to render their meaning precise. We simply refer to the common notion.

In engaging with this ‘lay concept’, researchers provided data to satisfy *political* curiosity and imperatives and sought to offer solutions to *political* problems. In other words *they themselves entered the political fray*. Drawing upon their armour of authority as knowledge producers and wielding the weapon of ‘objective’ knowledge, they too were attempting to shape the decisions taken by politicians. Some have also been rewarded with significant funding to carry out such research. As I bring this book to a close, I now want to expand further on why I think the dominant approach to knowing about public confidence in criminal justice ought to concern us.

6.2 ‘Costs to Existence’

Burchell (1996) has argued that we should look for the ‘costs to existence’ imposed by research by asking

> what sort of relationships with ourselves, others and the world does this way of speaking the truth presuppose, make possible and exclude? What other possibilities of existence are necessarily excluded, condemned, constrained? (34)

The use of quantitative polling to find out what the public think fails to open up a conversation with the participants and produces summaries of ‘*private* opinions’ which can come to be seen as natural facts (Bellah et al. 2008, 305). In its current form as a study of private opinions, the dominant strain in public confidence research is always partial and blinkered: it can only ‘hear’ certain things and not others as it delivers ‘facts’ in the authorised style. As argued in Chap. 3, to become visible to, and thus be understood and represented by, the survey, individuals must learn the ‘technique’ of being the kind of subject which the survey assumes they are: they must learn to ‘say’ what they think or feel in a way which is inevitably restricted, and they must submit to have their truncated expressions appropriated and transformed according to authorised ‘procedures of intervention’, or else they risk invisibility.

So, members of the public must evaluate or rate, choose or express a preference, estimate and, when they meet the requirements of the method in this way, their subjectivity may be appropriated and transformed—their selections may become ‘demands’, their preferences ‘desires’, their evaluations 'anger', and their estimations 'beliefs'. These new subjectivities can then become objects of policy: marketing, education, and so on. In this way, as individual citizens are subjected by the requirements of the survey method, they are also transformed from 'subjects of their own action into objects of intervention' (Bauman and May 2001, 169).

In societies where opinion surveys have come to be used on a regular, almost ubiquitous, basis, this ultimately has repercussions for public understandings of what politics is *and can be*. As Dryzek (1988) has observed:

> Every time a survey is designed, or its questionnaire administered, or its results analysed, or its conclusions reported in textbooks, or discussed by students in a class, or noted by fellow-practitioners, political leaders, or the attentive public, then a conception of politics as properly instrumental, individualistic, limited, reactive, and power-oriented is reinforced and furthered, at the expense of a politics of unimpeded discussion and interaction. (722)

These, then, are the 'costs to existence' of the dominant public confidence research agenda: a de-emphasising and restriction of opportunities for democratic engagement and dialogue between the public and policymakers that casts the public in the role of passive ill-informed *individual* consumers reliant upon the experts both to tell them how to know about crime and justice and to relay their 'real' opinions back to their elected representatives.

6.3 Towards a 'Better Politics'

> The mismeasure of political man lies squarely in the path of attempts to promote alternative visions of political life. (Dryzek 1988, 722)

My central objective in writing this book has been unashamedly normative. I fear for our shared future should currently dominant modes of political expression and engagement persist and I think it is important that social researchers, especially researchers concerned with matters of public opinion, recognise, and acknowledge the role that *their* efforts play in reinforcing particular ways of thinking about what is politically possible. With John Dryzek (1988, 2000), I would argue that viable political alternatives are being undermined by some social scientists who produce knowledge in a form that, however inadvertently and well-meaningly, nourishes a rather mean vision of the responsibilities and possibilities of democratic citizenship, at the expense of expanded and more positive alternatives.

Researchers should not, and indeed cannot, deny the political responsibilities that go along with researching any aspect of the so-called public opinion about the functioning of the democratic state and its agencies. Every time researchers engage in such research endeavours they insert themselves into, and thus necessarily begin to interfere with, the workings of democracy. Maintaining (or implying) the existence of a single knowable reality which is independent from and preceding the mechanisms they use to produce representations of that reality, and claiming that that pre-existing and objectively knowable reality *mandates* a particular approach to knowledge production, is a denial of their own entanglements within that reality. As Law (2004, 55) succinctly states:

> We are not dealing with different and possibly flawed perspectives on the same object. Rather we are dealing with different objects produced in different method assemblages.

Exploring whole 'method assemblages', as I have tried to do in this book with respect to 'public confidence in criminal justice', moves critique beyond a focus on how accurately researchers represent an implicitly singular and knowable reality to consider the social and political 'hinterlands' (cf. Law 2004) that render particular realities plausible. This allows us to focus with greater clarity on the ethical acceptability of the 'reality effects' the researchers leave in their wake and the 'costs to existence' they impose. I agree with Bourdieu's observation that 'we underestimate the properly political power to change social life by changing the representation of social life' (Bourdieu cited by Wacquant 2004, 3).

Knowledge producing and reporting activities both utilise and strengthen particular conceptions of society, and of the research subject, hailing individuals as consumers or citizens, and then assembling them into different kinds of publics: atomised, invisible to and uninterested in one another, or drawn into a communicative process which forces them to acknowledge and take each other into account. Those researchers who treat public confidence in the criminal justice system as a real object which is measurable, malleable, and *caused by* other external and measurable objects, construct subjects as individual consumers of public services, assemble atomised and non-deliberative publics, and thus circumscribe citizens' subjective potential and the legitimate avenues for political expression, contributing in their own way to a damaging 'suppression of … connectedness' (Lawler 2008, 149).

It does not seem to be too much of a leap from the above observations to suggest that survey-based research, neoliberal politics, and the 'opinionated habitus' are symbiotically entwined: neoliberalism is premised upon the notion of citizens as individual, preference holding consumers, survey researchers provide knowledge about public opinion (including public confidence) that reflects this understanding of the citizen, and citizens come to see this understanding of public opinion as commonplace and common sense, almost above questioning. Survey-based AGAP approaches to measuring public opinion, then, clearly occupy a strong position, both politically and socially: politically because they are congruent with neoliberal rationalities; and socially because they are compatible with a conception of 'public opinion' which has been internalised by citizens.

As I see it, then, the task for those of us who wish to see a 'better politics' emerge is to continually question and challenge claims made about public confidence and other aspects of public opinion based on survey-based AGAP research, and to insist that researchers fulfil their most fundamental responsibility: acknowledging fully the *value-based* choices they make (or allow others to make for them) about what to study and how (See Mills 2000).

Full recognition of the role played by values is essential here because, as this book has made clear, researchers of public confidence are not, despite what some might claim, engaged in objectively representing a pre-existing reality. Rather, they are actively contributing to the *actualisation* of a particular form of social and political reality. In assembling a public, however temporarily, whose opinion is to be in some way extracted through the research process, researchers are, in some sense, creating both a social experience (that of having one's opinion researched) and a picture of society which may be reflected back into that society. They are involved in the making of political worlds. That is the central claim that this book has sought to illuminate. It has tried to do this by making an example of an area of research of particular relevance to the academic field within which I primarily teach and research: criminology. But the more general normative conclusion that it leads me towards is more broadly applicable. Researchers should not hide behind (or be suffered by their peers to hide behind) an objectivist epistemology in order to avoid acknowledging their objectives and responsibilities as inevitably political actors. As Foucault (1994, 32) observed: 'Political power is not absent from knowledge, it is woven together with it.'

References

Bauman, Zygmunt, and Tim May. 2001. *Thinking Sociologically*. Oxford: Blackwell.

Bellah, R.N., R. Madsen, W. Sullivan, A. Swidler, and S.M. Tipton. 2008. *Habits of the Heart: Individualism and Commitment in American Life*. Berkley: University of California Press.

Burchell, Graham. 1996. Liberal Government and Techniques of the Self. In *Foucault and Political Reason: Liberalism, Neo-liberalism and Rationalities of Government*, ed. A. Barry, T. Osborne, and N. Rose, 19–36. London: Routledge.

Dryzek, John S. 1988. The Mismeasure of Political Man. *Journal of Politics* 50: 705–725.

———. 2000. *Deliberative Democracy and Beyond: Liberals, Critics, Contestations*. Oxford: Oxford University Press.

Durkheim, Emile. 1938. *The Rules of Sociological Method*. New York: The Free Press.

Foucault, Michel. 1994. Truth and Juridical Forms. In *Power*, ed. James D. Faubion, 1–9. New York: The New York Press.

Giddens, A. 1990. *The Consequences of Modernity*. Cambridge: Polity Press.

Law, John. 2004. *After Method: Mess in Social Science Research*. Abingdon: Routledge.

Lawler, S. 2008. *Identity*. Cambridge: Polity Press.

Mills, C. Wright. 2000. *The Sociological Imagination*. Oxford: Oxford University Press.

Wacquant, Loic. 2004. Pointers on Pierre Bourdieu and Democratic Politics. *Constellations* 11 (1): 3–15.

Appendix 1: A More Detailed Description and Critique of Some Studies of Public Confidence Completed in the Early 2000s

Locally Commissioned Studies

As noted in the Preface to this book, from 2006 to 2009 I worked as a 'KTP Associate' on a project designed to help local criminal justice agencies respond to the public confidence target. In this role I attended meetings of individuals working for Local Criminal Justice Boards, which were focused on matters to do with marketing, communications, and community engagement and tended to be the 'go to' people in terms of work to increase public confidence. Through the contacts I gained I was provided with a number of reports on research carried out to try and understand public confidence better which were not in more general circulation. These included:

- Addison, M. 2006. Public Confidence in the Criminal Justice System. Newcastle Upon Tyne: Dipsticks Research.
- Devon and Cornwall Police. 2007. Baseline Survey: December 2006. Exeter: Devon and Cornwall Criminal Justice Board.
- Dodgson, M. 2006. Shaping Public Confidence in the Criminal Justice System. Newcastle upon Tyne, UK: Dr. Marina Dodgson, Research and Consultancy.
- Dodgson, M; Dodgson, R and O'Donnell, A. 2006. Shaping Public Confidence in the Criminal Justice System: Literature Review. Newcastle Upon Tyne: Dr. Marina Dodgson, Research and Consultancy.

E.R. Turner, *Public Confidence in Criminal Justice*,
Critical Criminological Perspectives,
https://doi.org/10.1007/978-3-319-67897-9

- Greater Manchester Police. 2005. Greater Manchester Citizens' Panel—Survey Results March 2005. Manchester, UK: Greater Manchester Police.
- Holme, M. 2006. Cumbria Citizen's Panel Survey 2006. Penrith, UK: Cumbria Criminal Justice Board.
- Opinion Leader Research. 2005. Confidence Levels of Black and Minority Groups in the Criminal Justice System in Thames Valley. London, UK: Opinion Leader Research.

As noted in Chap. 2, the influence of local research on the dominant knowledge discourse of confidence appears to have been limited as most of it was reported locally, but not subsequently cited elsewhere. The research tended to replicate the approaches used in the national-level research, rediscovering on a 'local' basis knowledge about confidence that is already in circulation. For a more detailed discussion, see Turner (2008).

MORI

MORI carried out research in which '[t]he public's attitudes and perceptions of the system and its constituent agencies ... were measured to identify the factors relating to levels of confidence and satisfaction' (Page et al. 2004, 1). The MORI study positioned itself as making a further contribution to the body of knowledge on public confidence in the criminal justice system (CJS), and this is the context in which it has been subsequently cited. It had a robust data collection mechanism, using a random-sample telephone survey. The analysis managed to be both self-confident: 'confidence in the system overall ... *would* increase' (Page et al. 2004, 6, emphasis added); and yet also vague and obvious: 'creating a society where people feel safe and dealing effectively with violent crime' (Page et al. 2004, 6). It used a different measure of confidence from that used within the British Crime Survey (BCS),[1] and approached the matter of public knowledge differently.[2]

Some of the conclusions in the MORI study appear to have been drawn based on rather opaque and questionable analytical manoeuvres. For example, data on confidence and knowledge were aggregated to analyse the relationship between these two variables on an agency-by-agency basis: the average score which respondents gave to their 'familiarity' with each agency was plotted against the average score which they gave each agency for its 'effect on crime'. These points were found to make a reasonably clear diagonal line on a graph but no indication of the statistical significance of the relationship was given. It is not clear why the researchers chose to plot aggregated data on this graph, rather than plotting data points for each individual respondent and calculating the correlation coefficient for the relationship between perceived importance and perceived effectiveness of the different functions.

The report also includes a graph which plots the proportion of respondents who see certain functions of the CJS as 'absolutely essential' against the proportion who have confidence that they are being delivered. The authors highlighted five functions of the CJS which, they said, were seen by a majority of respondents as being 'absolutely essential' and in which a relatively low proportion of respondents said they had confidence.[3] These points were ringed on the graph to provide visual emphasis of their importance (Page et al. 2004, 3). They were also referred to again in the conclusion, which stated that these issues should 'be regarded as public priorities for addressing confidence in the criminal justice system' (Page et al. 2004, 6). The basis upon which this prescription is made is tenuous to say the least, as a number of other functions were on the periphery of the seemingly arbitrarily drawn circle on the graph (one of these issues was 'tackling the causes of crime'). Bearing these points in mind the selection of the key issues to be addressed has more than a suspicion of arbitrariness, if not bias.

NOP World/Phillip Gould Associates

The NOP World/PGA study used a qualitative approach with a relatively small sample of approximately 50 respondents which was, by their own admission, not representative, and which they regarded as a pilot study (NOP World 2003, 7). Despite these limitations the final presentation of their findings ran to 108 PowerPoint slides and adopted a confident and authoritative tone throughout. Its recommendations included ensuring that legislation put victims before criminals, and 'breaking through media distortion' by communicating to the public that sentences are 'longer, tougher, more consistent' (NOP World 2003, 107).

Controlled Experiments

The first such study (Chapman et al. 2002) was initiated in response to the concerns which arose because of a review of the sentencing framework during 2000/2001. Doubts were expressed about using public opinion to inform the review in light of knowledge about the extent of public 'misperceptions' about crime and justice.[4] In response, an investigation was commissioned to explore whether such misperceptions could be corrected by improving knowledge, and whether improved knowledge would impact upon views. It was felt that such an investigation could also be of value in helping with progress towards the newly imposed target of increasing public confidence in the CJS:

> In theory… improving public knowledge about crime, sentencing and the CJS might be expected to result in more positive attitudes towards the CJS. Improvements in ratings of the system should be achievable where current opinion is based on overly negative beliefs. (Chapman et al. 2002, 2–3)

Chapman et al. found that '[k]nowledge of crime trends and current sentencing practice is particularly poor, with only about one in ten people being *reasonably well-informed* in these areas' (Ibid., 9, emphasis added). What constitutes being 'reasonably well-informed' is not explicitly defined; however, the approach adopted indicates that, as Chapman et al. concede, knowledgeability boils down to 'recall of key facts' (Ibid., 15).[5] In their experiment, they claim to have been able to improve 'recall of key facts' through the provision of information but, although the confidence of about a third of participants increased, 'there was no clear relationship between improved scores on the knowledge questions and improved levels of confidence' (Ibid., 35).

Salisbury (2004) built on the previous body of research and the experimental work carried out by Chapman et al. (2002) by providing a booklet to a sample of BCS respondents and conducting a follow-up interview two weeks later to see if their views had changed. A control group did not receive the booklet but still had a follow-up interview. Salisbury found that having received and at least glanced through the booklet increased the accuracy of people's perception of crime trends, but not of criminal justice practice. However, the research concluded that increases in confidence could not be attributed to the impact of looking at the booklet or to increased awareness about crime and criminal justice.[6]

Singer and Cooper (2008) sought to update and improve upon these experimental studies[7] by exploring the relative effectiveness of different methods of providing information. Their approach to the design of the informational materials drew on marketing theory and sought to 'inform, persuade and remind' the recipient about key facts. Their peer-reviewed[8] study demonstrated that statistically significant increases in the accuracy of public estimations of crime trends and certain facets of criminal justice practice could be achieved, at least in the short term, through the delivery of a carefully designed information booklet. The research also indicated that statistically significant increases in confidence (as measured by the general confidence measure from the BCS) could be achieved in the short term.

However, although the researchers found statistically significant differences between the control group and the experimental group (those receiving the booklet), they rather overstated the magnitude of the effect. The research found that the proportion of the control group who were confident that the CJS is effective increased 6.7 percentage points between the first and second interview, whilst the proportion of the experimental group who were confident that the CJS is effective increased by 11.4 percentage points. Based on this finding, the authors claimed that 'a professionally designed booklet delivered through a personalised envelope or personal contact is a *very effective* way of raising public confidence in the CJS' (Ibid., 20, *emphasis added*). The percentage point gain of the experimental group over the control was 4.7 percentage points. Sufficient effect magnitude for us to reject the null hypothesis, but to say that the intervention was 'very effective' seems somewhat misleading. Furthermore, the increase in confidence was only significantly different compared to the control group where the booklet was handed to the recipient as opposed to 'delivered through a personalized envelope'.

The authors also notably fail to emphasise that of those who received the booklet only 40% actually read all or most of it and (unlike in the earlier study by Salisbury (2004)) there was no analysis of whether improvements in knowledge and confidence were seen even in those who received but did not read the booklet. It is therefore unclear whether it was the content of the booklet, or simply the fact of receiving a booklet, which produced the change in knowledge and confidence. It seems, then, that the authors may have been tempted to oversell the import of their findings, perhaps cognisant of the observation by Tonry and Green (2003, 494) that 'qualified claims about modest but discernible sought-after effects, important though they are, seldom support a sense of excitement likely to lead to major new initiatives or changes in policy direction.' Furthermore, although the study aimed to provide usable evidence for local practitioners one thing which is entirely missing is any information on the costs associated with the design, production, and distribution of the booklet. The reader cannot, therefore, know the cost of producing the relatively modest (and potentially fleeting) percentage increases in knowledge and confidence which the study claims.

Notes

1. The MORI study focused on how confident respondents were 'about the way that crime is dealt with' at the local and national levels (Page et al. 2004, 2).
2. The study asked respondents how much they felt they knew about the different agencies and then what effect they thought each agency had on crime in their area.
3. These were the following: creating a society where people feel safe, reducing the level of crime, stopping offenders from committing more crime, dealing effectively with street robbery (including mugging), bringing people who commit crimes to justice.
4. As discussed in Chap. 2, in the 1970s and 1980s many researchers expressed the opinion that the lack of public knowledge about crime and justice completely undermined the validity of general measures of opinion. They proposed instead the use of specific sentencing scenarios to elicit public preferences. It is interesting that less than 20 years later the preferred option is to attempt to manipulate general opinion through education, rather than to capture it in a different, and arguably more appropriate, way.
5. The authors contrast public perceptions of key statistics, with the actual figures, generating findings such as '[e]ight in ten respondents thought half or less of adult male burglars were given custodial sentences, although the actual proportion for 1999 was 72 per cent.' (Chapman et al 2002, 9). In other words, to be well informed appears to mean being able to give accurate estimations of criminal justice statistics.
6. 'Increases in confidence were not restricted to only those who received the booklet [and thus] were not solely attributable to looking at the booklet' (Salisbury 2004, 11). Furthermore, '[t]here was a significant increase in the proportion feeling that the sentences handed down by the courts are about right (from 15% to 25%) for those who received and looked at the booklet. However, there was also a significant increase (from 20% to 34%) for those who did not receive the booklet' (Salisbury 2004, 12). Salisbury also found that respondents who thought that taking part in the BCS had made them more aware of crime and criminal justice issues were no more likely than those who did not feel more aware to have increased in confidence (Salisbury 2004, 12).
7. Unlike Chapman et al. (2002) and Salisbury (2004), Singer and Cooper (2008), avoid committing the statistical error of failing to test the statistical significance of the differences between control and experimental groups. It is not statistically correct to claim that there is a difference between the groups unless this difference has been tested for significance (see Bland 2000).

8. The Home Office operates its own peer-reviewing system, the rigour of which has been critiqued by Hope (2008).
9. A search on the term 'criminal justice system' revealed that, in the British Library database of British Newspapers 1600–1900, the phrase did not occur at all, whilst in the *Times* newspaper, the term was not used in relation to Britain until 1973. Uses of the term during the 1970s were sparsely distributed and tended to be with reference to the US context (particularly the Watergate affair) or appeared to be prompted by, and often directly quoting from, academic or other research reports, or the words of the researchers themselves. The idea of criminal justice operating as a system, and thus the application of the term 'criminal justice system' began to become more prominent during the 1980s (See Bottoms 1995, 24).

References

Bland, M. 2000. *An Introduction to Medical Statistics*. Oxford: Oxford University Press.

Chapman, Becca, Catriona Mirrlees-Black, and Claire Brawn. 2002. *Improving Public Attitudes to the Criminal Justice System: The Impact of Information*. London: Home Office.

Hope, T. 2008. A Firing Squad to Shoot the Messenger: Home Office Peer Review of Research. In *Critical Thinking About the Uses of Research*, ed. R Walters and T Hope, 27–44. London: Centre for Crime and Justice Studies.

NOP World. 2003. *Drivers of Confidence in the Criminal Justice System*. London, UK: Home Office.

Page, B., R. Wake, and A. Ames. 2004. *Home Office Findings 221: Public Confidence in the Criminal Justice System*. London: Home Office.

Roberts, Julian V., Loretta J. Stalans, David Indermaur, and Mike Hough. 2003. *Penal Populism and Public Opinion: Lessons from Five Countries*. Oxford: Oxford University Press.

Salisbury, Heather. 2004. *Public Attitudes to the Criminal Justice System: The Impact of Providing Information to British Crime Survey Respondents*. London: Home Office.

Singer, Lawrence, and Suzanne Cooper. 2008. *Inform, Persuade and Remind: An Evaluation of a Project to Improve Public Confidence in the Criminal Justice System*. London: Ministry of Justice.

Tonry, M., and D. Green. 2003. Criminology and Public Policy in the USA and UK. In *The Criminological Foundations of Penal Policy*, ed. Lucia Zedner, Andrew Ashworth. Oxford: Oxford University Press.

Appendix 2: Approaching the Genealogical Analysis of Public Confidence

Using the search engines of the Times Digital Archive and the Lexis Nexis digital archive of the *Guardian* and the *Times/Sunday Times* I carried out a quantitative content analysis to gain an initial overview of the prevalence and historical distribution of the term 'public confidence' used in relation to criminal justice matters within the print media. I found that the term public confidence occurred much more frequently in the last quarter of the twentieth century than at any time prior to this. Mentions of 'public confidence' in parliamentary debates also showed a definite upwards trend in the last two decades of the twentieth century, suggesting that at least some of the increase in use of the term public confidence in the newspapers reflected the increasing political salience of the term. In both the *Times* and the *Guardian* Newspapers there was a generally upward trend in use of the term 'public confidence' in each five-year period from 1985 to 2004.

Next I searched to see how many times the term 'public confidence' occurred along with either 'police' or 'justice'. I searched for all articles using the term 'public confidence' where one of the article keywords was either 'justice' or 'police'. The results of this search for each 50-year period from 1785 to 1984 are displayed in Table 1, below. These figures suggest that the notion of public confidence in justice had virtually no presence in the content of the *Times* newspaper prior to 1985, whilst the notion of public confidence in police had a limited presence from the late nineteenth century onwards, and became more frequently used during the twentieth century.

E.R. Turner, *Public Confidence in Criminal Justice*,
Critical Criminological Perspectives,
https://doi.org/10.1007/978-3-319-67897-9

Table 1 Frequency of use of 'public confidence' in relation to justice/police in the *Times* 1785–1984

	1785–1834	*1835–1884*	*1885–1934*	*1935–1984*
Justice	1 (<1%)	3 (<1%)	8 (<1%)	19 (<1%)
Police	0 (0%)	7 (<1%)	21 (1%)	105 (5%)

Percentages displayed correspond to frequency expressed as a percentage of all mentions of 'public confidence'

Table 2 Frequency of occurrence of 'public confidence' in same sentence as justice/police 1984–2009

		1984–1989	*1989–1994*	*1994–1999*	*1999–2004*	*2004–2009*
Justice	*Times*	25 (5%)	64 (10%)	57 (8%)	83 (10%)	102 (11%)
	Guardian	26 (8%)	57 (14%)	37 (6%)	37 (6%)	40 (7%)
Police	*Times*	22 (5%)	86 (14%)	33 (5%)	46 (6%)	55 (6%)
	Guardian	42 (13%)	55 (13%)	45 (8%)	24 (4%)	42 (7%)

Percentages displayed correspond to frequency expressed as a percentage of all mentions of 'public confidence'

Table 2 (below) displays usage of 'public confidence' in the same sentence as the words 'police' or 'justice' in the *Times/Sunday Times* and the *Guardian* newspapers since 1984. These figures were obtained from the Lexis Nexis search engine. As can be seen, both in crude volume terms and in proportion to other uses of the term 'public confidence', there was a spike in the use of 'public confidence' in the same sentence as 'justice' or 'police' between 1989 and 1994. Analysing each of these years individually I found that during that five-year period the prevalence (numerical and proportional) of the term 'public confidence' used in the same sentence as the word police was at its peak in both newspapers in 1989 and 1990, but declined thereafter, whereas the prevalence (numerical and proportional) of the term 'public confidence' used in the same sentence as the word justice was highest between 1991 and 1993. In the *Guardian* in 1993, 21% of uses of the term 'public confidence' came in the same sentence as the word justice (18 articles in all).

Using the Lexis Nexis database I then counted how many articles from the *Times/Sunday Times* and the *Guardian* contained the specific phrase 'public confidence in the criminal justice system' in each year from 1985 to 2009.

The results indicate that the phrase only came into common usage in the media from 1992 onwards. It seems that during earlier periods the term 'public confidence in the administration of justice' was preferred, reflecting the fact that the term 'criminal justice system' was not widely used in relation to England and Wales prior to the 1970s.[9] Indeed, it was not until 1982 that the term 'public confidence in the criminal justice system' featured in media discourse, as the *Times* reported a speech in the House of Commons by the then Home Secretary William Whitelaw. The term had in fact first been used in parliamentary debate the previous year when Ivan Lawrence MP referred to it in relation to proposals by the Royal Commission on Criminal Procedure (1981) to establish an independent prosecution service. Usage of the term in debates was sparse in the 1980s, became much more prevalent in the mid-1990s, and had a significant spike in 2003/2004. Furthermore, the figures showed that the term was used much more frequently within parliamentary debates than it was in the content of the *Times* and the *Guardian* newspapers.

Using various digitised archival sources then, I was able to note that the use of the term 'public confidence' in relation to the issue of justice was virtually non-existent in *Times* newspaper content prior to the early 1980s. I was also able to identify 1981 as the first year in which the phrase 'public confidence in the criminal justice system' was used in a parliamentary debate, and 1982 as the first time that a discourse of 'public confidence' came together with that of the 'criminal justice system' in *Times* newspaper content. I also identified 1989–1994 as the period during which the use of the term 'public confidence' in the same sentence as justice or police became more frequent in newspaper content, and I identified a spike in the use of the term 'public confidence' in relation to police in 1989 and 1990, and a spike in the use of the term 'public confidence' in relation to justice from 1991 to 1993. The phrase 'public confidence in the criminal justice system' was most prevalent in newspaper content in 1992–1994, 1996–1997, 2000, 2003 and 2007. In parliamentary debates this exact phrase became more frequent between 1994 and 1997, in 2000 and between 2002 and 2004.

Gaining this quantitative overview of the historical content of the *Times* and the *Guardian* newspapers and parliamentary debates enabled me to familiarise myself with the data, to identify the newspaper articles and political debates which would form my sample for more detailed qualitative analysis, and to identify key points in time in the history of 'public confidence in the criminal justice system'. To start the qualitative analytical process, I reviewed every newspaper article since 1982 which contained the phrase 'public confidence in the criminal justice system'. I coded these according to how and why confidence had been invoked in each of these articles (the material events and conditions it referred to), and any links which the article made to other texts (its intertextual relations). After this point, the selection and analysis of further texts was a perambulatory process: as I identified events and texts of interest so I used these to search for other texts, all the time building up a sense of the points at which confidence entered (or did not enter) and was transmitted through the discourse. The purpose of this journey through linked events and texts (a journey into the discourse) was to apply the Foucauldian strategy of 'eventalization':

> making visible a singularity at places where there is a temptation to invoke a historical constant, an immediate anthropological trait, or an obviousness which imposes itself uniformly on all. To show that things "weren't as necessary as all that" (Foucault 1991, 73)

References

Bottoms, Anthony. 1995. The Philosophy and Politics of Punishment and Sentencing. In *The Politics of Sentencing Reform*, ed. Chris Clarkson and Rod Morgan, 17–49. Oxford: Clarendon Press.

Foucault, M. 1991. Questions of Method. In *The Foucault Effect: Studies in Governmentality*, ed. Peter Miller, Colin Gordon, Graham Burchell, 73–86. Chicago: University of Chicago Press.

Bibliography

Ackerman, Bruce, and James S. Fishkin. 2004. *Deliberation Day*. New Haven: Yale University Press.
Addison, M. 2006. *Public Confidence in the Criminal Justice System*. Newcastle Upon Tyne: Dipsticks Research.
Allen, R. 2002. "There Must Be Some Way of Dealing with Kids": Young Offenders, Public Attitudes and Policy Change. *Youth Justice* 2: 3–13.
———. 2004. What Works in Changing Public Attitudes: Lessons from Rethinking Crime and Punishment. *Journal for Crime, Conflict and the Media* 1 (3): 55–67.
Allen, J., M. El Komy, J. Lovbakke, and H. Roy. 2005. *Policing and the Criminal Justice System – Public Confidence and Perceptions: Findings from the 2003/04 British Crime Survey*. London: Home Office.
Banks, C., E. Maloney, and H. Willcock. 1975. Public Attitudes to Crime and the Penal System. *British Journal of Criminology* 15 (3): 228–240.
Bauman, Z. 1987. *Legislators and Interpreters*. Cambridge: Polity.
Bauman, Zygmunt, and Tim May. 2001. *Thinking Sociologically*. Oxford: Blackwell.
Beattie, J. 1986. *Crime and the Courts in England 1660–1800*. Oxford: Clarendon.
Bell, Emma. 2011. *Criminal Justice and Neoliberalism*. Houndmills: Palgrave Macmillan.
———. 2014. There Is an Alternative: Challenging the Logic of Neoliberal Penality. *Theoretical Criminology* 18 (4): 489–505.
Bellah, R.N., R. Madsen, W. Sullivan, A. Swidler, and S.M. Tipton. 2008. *Habits of the Heart: Individualism and Commitment in American Life*. Berkley/Los Angeles: University of California Press.

E.R. Turner, *Public Confidence in Criminal Justice*,
Critical Criminological Perspectives,
https://doi.org/10.1007/978-3-319-67897-9

Beniger, James R. 1992. The Impact of Polling on Public Opinion: Reconciling Foucault, Habermas, and Bourdieu. *International Journal of Public Opinion Research* 4 (3): 204–219.

Bosworth, Mary. 2011. Penal Moderation in the United States? Yes We Can. *Criminology & Public Policy* 10 (2): 335–343.

Bottoms, Anthony. 1995. The Philosophy and Politics of Punishment and Sentencing. In *The Politics of Sentencing Reform*, ed. Chris Clarkson and Rod Morgan, 17–49. Oxford: Clarendon.

Bourdieu, Pierre. 1984. *Distinction: A Social Critique of the Judgement of Taste*. London: Routledge.

Brereton, David. 1996. Does Criminology Matter? Crime, Politics and the Policy Process. *Current Issues in Criminal Justice* 8 (1): 82–88.

Burchell, Graham. 1996. Liberal Government and Techniques of the Self. In *Foucault and Political Reason: Liberalism, Neo-liberalism and Rationalities of Government*, ed. A. Barry, T. Osborne, and N. Rose, 19–36. London: Routledge.

Butler, Lord. 1974. The Foundation of the Institute of Criminology in Cambridge. In *Crime, Criminology and Public Policy*, ed. R. Hood, 1–10. London: Heineman.

Carrabine, J. 2001. Unmarried Motherhood 1830–1990: A Genealogical Analysis. In *Discourse as Data: A Guide for Analysis*, ed. Margaret Wetherell, Stephanie Taylor, and Simeon J. Yates, 267–310. London: Sage.

Casey, L. 2008. *Engaging Communities in Fighting Crime*. London: Cabinet Office.

Chapman, Becca, Catriona Mirrlees-Black, and Claire Brawn. 2002. *Improving Public Attitudes to the Criminal Justice System: The Impact of Information*. London: Home Office.

Devon and Cornwall Police. 2007. *Baseline Survey: December 2006*. Exeter: Devon and Cornwall Criminal Justice Board.

Dodgson, M. 2006. *Shaping Public Confidence in the Criminal Justice System*. Newcastle upon Tyne: Dr. Marina Dodgson, Research and Consultancy.

Dodgson, M., R. Dodgson, and A. O'Donnell. 2006. *Shaping Public Confidence in the Criminal Justice System: Literature Review*. Newcastle Upon Tyne: Dr. Marina Dodgson, Research and Consultancy.

Doob, Anthony N., and Julian V. Roberts. 1984. Social Psychology, Social Attitudes, and Attitudes Towards Sentencing. *Canadian Journal of Behavioural Science* 16 (4): 269–280.

———. 1988. Public Punitiveness and Public Knowledge of the Facts: Some Canadian Surveys. In *Public Attitudes to Sentencing: Surveys from Five Countries*, ed. N. Walker and M. Hough, 111–133. Aldershot: Gower.

Downes, David, and Rod Morgan. 1997. Dumping the "Hostages to Fortune"? The Politics of Law and Order in Post-War Britain. In *The Oxford Handbook of Criminology*, ed. M. Maguire, R. Morgan, and R. Reiner, 87–134. Oxford: Oxford University Press.

Drury, J. 2002. "When the Mobs are Looking for Witches to Burn, Nobody's Safe": Talking about the Reactionary Crowd. *Discourse and Society* 13 (1): 41–73.

Dryzek, John S. 1988. The Mismeasure of Political Man. *Journal of Politics* 50: 705–725.

———. 2000. *Deliberative Democracy and Beyond: Liberals, Critics, Contestations.* Oxford: Oxford University Press.

Duffy, B., R. Wake, T. Burrows, and P. Bremner. 2007. *Closing the Gaps: Crime and Public Perceptions.* London: Ipsos MORI.

Durkheim, Emile. 1938. *The Rules of Sociological Method.* New York: The Free Press.

Dzur, Albert W. 2012. *Punishment, Participatory Democracy and the Jury.* Oxford: Oxford University Press.

Dzur, A.W., and R. Mirchandi. 2007. Punishment and Democracy: The Role of public Deliberation. *Punishment and Society* 9 (2): 151–175.

Emsley, C. 1987. *Crime and Society in England 1750–1900.* Harlow: Longman.

Fairclough, Nigel. 2003. *Analysing Discourse: Textual Analysis for Social Research.* London: Routledge.

Fielding, Nigel, and Martin Innes. 2006. Reassurance Policing, Community Policing and Measuring Police Performance. *Policing and Society* 16 (2): 127–145.

Fishkin, James S. 1995. *The Voice of the People: Public Opinion and Democracy.* New Haven: Yale University Press.

Fishkin, J. 1996. Bringing Deliberation to Democracy. *The Public Perspective* 7 (1): 1–4.

Flanagan, Sir Ronnie. 2008. *The Review of Policing: Final Report.* London: Home Office.

Foucault, M. 1972. *The Archaeology of Knowledge.* Trans. A.M. Sheridan Smith. London: Tavistock.

———. 1977. *Discipline and Punish: The Birth of the Prison.* London: Allen Lane.

———. 1991a. Governmentality. In *The Foucault Effect: Studies in Governmentality*, ed. G. Burchell, C. Gordon, and P. Miller, 87–104. Chicago: Chicago University Press.

———. 1991b. Questions of Method. In *The Foucault Effect: Studies in Governmentality*, ed. Peter Miller, Colin Gordon, and Graham Burchell, 73–86. Chicago: University of Chicago Press.

———. 1994. Truth and Juridical Forms. In *Power*, ed. James D. Faubion, 1–9. New York: The New York Press.

Freiberg, Arie. 2001. Affective Versus Effective Justice: Instrumentalism and Emotionalism in Criminal Justice. *Punishment and Society* 3 (2): 265–278.

Garland, D. 1990. *Punishment and Modern Society.* Oxford: Oxford University Press.

———. 1996. The Limits of the Sovereign State: Strategies of Crime Control in Contemporary Society. *The British Journal of Criminology* 36 (4): 445–471.

———. 2000. The Culture of High Crime Societies: Some Preconditions of Recent 'Law and Order' Policies. *British Journal of Criminology* 40 (2): 347–375.

———. 2001. *The Culture of Control*. Oxford: Oxford University Press.

Garland, D., and R. Sparks. 2000. Criminology, Social Theory and the Challenge of Our Times. In *Criminology and Social Theory*, ed. Richard Sparks and David W. Garland, 1–22. Oxford: Oxford University Press.

Garofalo, J. 1977. *Public Opinion About Crime: The Attitudes of Victims and Nonvictims in Selected Cities*. Albany: US Department of Justice.

Giddens, A. 1990. *The Consequences of Modernity*. Cambridge: Polity Press.

Girling, Evi, Ian Loader, and Richard Sparks. 2000. *Crime and Social Change in Middle England*. London: Routledge.

Greater Manchester Police. 2005. *Greater Manchester Citizens' Panel – Survey Results March 2005*. Manchester: Greater Manchester Police.

Green, David A. 2006. Public Opinion Versus Public Judgment About Crime: Correcting the 'Comedy of Errors'. *British Journal of Criminology* 46: 131–154.

———. 2008. *When Children Kill Children: Penal Populism and Political Culture*. Oxford: Oxford University Press.

Grimshaw, R. 2004. *Whose Justice? Principal Drivers of Criminal Justice Policy, Their Implications for Stakeholders, and Some Foundations for Critical Policy Departures*. Selected Papers from the 2004 British Criminology Conference, Portsmouth July 2004, http://www.britsoccrim.org/v7.htm. Accessed 30 Nov 2009.

Hacking, I. 1991. How Should We Do the History of Statistics? In *The Foucault Effect: Studies in Governmentality*, ed. Graham Burchell, Peter M. Miller, and Colin Gordon, 181–196. Chicago: University of Chicago Press.

Hallsworth, Simon. 2000. Rethinking the Punitive Turn: Economies of Excess and the Criminology of the Other. *Punishment and Society* 2 (2): 145–160.

Hammersley, M. 1995. *The Politics of Social Research*. London: Sage.

Hanway, J. 1775. *The Defects of Police, the Cause of Immorality and the Continual Robberies Committed, Particularly in the Metropolis*. London: J Dodsley.

Hill, C. 1972. *The World Turned Upside Down: Radical Ideas During the English Revolution*. London: Temple Smith.

Hindelang, M.J. 1974. Public Opinion Regarding Crime, Criminal Justice and Related Topics. *Journal of Research in Crime and Delinquency* 11 (2): 101–116.

Holme, M. 2006. *Cumbria Citizen's Panel Survey 2006*. Penrith: Cumbria Criminal Justice Board.

Hood, C. 1991. A Public Management for All Seasons? *Public Administration* 69: 3–19.

Hopkins-Burke, R. 2009. *An Introduction to Criminological Theory*. Cullompton: Willan.

Hough, Mike. 2003. Modernization and Public Opinion: Some Criminal Justice Paradoxes. *Contemporary Politics* 9 (2): 143–155.

Hough, Mike, and Patricia Mayhew. 1983. *The British Crime Survey: First Report.* London: Her Majesty's Stationary Office.

———. 1985. *Taking Account of Crime: Key Findings From the Second British Crime Survey.* London: Home Office.

Hough, Mike, and David Moxon. 1985. Dealing with Offenders: Popular Opinion and the Views of Victims – Findings from the British Crime Survey. *The Howard Journal* 24 (3): 160–175.

Hough, Mike, and Alison Park. 2002. How Malleable Are Attitudes to Crime and Punishment? Findings from a British Deliberative Poll. In *Changing Attitudes to Punishment: Public Opinion, Crime and Justice*, ed. J.V. Roberts and M. Hough, 163–183. Cullompton: Willan.

Hough, Mike, and Julian V. Roberts. 1998. *Attitudes to Punishment: Findings from the British Crime Survey.* London: Home Office.

Hughes, J.A., and W.W. Sharrock. 2007. *Theory and Methods in Sociology: An Introduction to Sociological Thinking and Practice.* Basingstoke: Palgrave Macmillan.

Hunter, J. 2010. *The Making of the Crofting Community.* Edinburgh: Birlinn.

Jackson, J., and J. Sunshine. 2007. Public Confidence in Policing: A Neo-Durkheimian Perspective. *British Journal of Criminology* 47 (2): 214–233.

Jones, T., B. MacLean, and J. Young. 1986. *The Islington Crime Survey.* Aldershot: Gower.

Kendall, G., and G. Whickham. 1999. *Using Foucault's Methods.* London: Sage.

Law, John. 2004. *After Method: Mess in Social Science Research.* Abingdon: Routledge.

Lawler, S. 2008. *Identity.* Cambridge: Polity Press.

Lee, Murray. 2007. *Inventing Fear of Crime: Criminology and the Politics of Anxiety.* Cullompton: Willan.

Loader, I. 2006. Fall of the 'Platonic Guardians': Liberalism, Criminology and Political Responses to Crime in England and Wales. *British Journal of Criminology* 46: 561–586.

———. 2008. The Anti-politics of Crime. *Theoretical Criminology* 12 (3): 399–410.

———. 2010. For Penal Moderation: Notes Towards a Public Philosophy of Punishment. *Theoretical Criminology* 14 (3): 349–367.

———. 2011. Playing with Fire? Democracy and the Emotions of Crime and Punishment. In *Emotions, Crime and Justice*, ed. Susanne Karstedt, Ian Loader, and Heather Strang, 347–362. Oxford: Hart.

Loader, I., and R. Sparks. 2010. Wacquant and Civic Sociology: "Formative Intentions" and Formative Experiences. *Criminology and Criminal Justice* 10 (4): 405–415.

———. 2011a. Criminology and Democratic Politics: A Reply to Critics. *British Journal of Criminology* 51 (4): 734–738.
———. 2011b. *Public Criminology?* London: Routledge.
———. 2012. Beyond Lamentation: Towards a Democratic Egalitarian Politics of Crime and Justice. In *Policing: Politics, Culture and Control*, ed. T. Newburn and J. Peay, 11–42. Oxford: Hart Publishing.
Lodge, T.S. 1974. The Founding of the Home Office Research Unit. In *Crime, Criminology and Public Policy*, ed. R. Hood, 11–24. London: Heinemann.
Lupton, D., and J. Tulloch. 1999. Theorizing Fear of Crime: Beyond the Rational/Irrational Opposition. *British Journal of Sociology* 50 (3): 507–523.
Luskin, Robert C., James S. Fishkin, and Roger Jowell. 2002. Considered Opinions: Deliberative Polling in Britain. *British Journal of Political Science* 32: 455–487.
Matthews, R. 2009. Beyond 'So What?' Criminology: Rediscovering Realism. *Theoretical Criminology* 13 (3): 341–362.
Mattinson, Joanna, and Catriona Mirrlees-Black. 2000. *Attitudes to Crime and Criminal Justice: Findings from the 1998 British Crime Survey*. London: Home Office.
Mills, C. Wright. 2000. *The Sociological Imagination*. Oxford: Oxford University Press.
Mirrlees-Black, Catriona. 2001. *Confidence in the Criminal Justice System: Findings from the 2000 British Crime Survey*. London: Home Office.
Moore, Sir. E. 1899. *Liverpool in King Charles the Second's Time*. Liverpool: Henry Young and Sons.
NOP World. 2003. *Drivers of Confidence in the Criminal Justice System*. London: Home Office.
O'Farrell, Clare. 2005. *Michel Foucault*. London: Sage.
O'Malley, P. 1999. Volatile and Contradictory Punishment. *Theoretical Criminology* 3 (2): 175–196.
Opinion Leader Research. 2005. *Confidence Levels of Black and Minority Groups in the Criminal Justice System in Thames Valley*. London: Opinion Leader Research.
Ormrod, The Hon. Sir Roger. 1964. The Developing Relations Between the Law and the Social Sciences. *British Journal of Criminology* 4 (4): 320–331.
Osborne, T., and N. Rose. 1999. Do the Social Sciences Create Phenomena: The Case of Public Opinion Research. *British Journal of Sociology* 50 (3): 367–396.
Pasquino, P. 1991. Criminology: The Birth of a Special Knowledge. In *The Foucault Effect: Studies in Governmentality*, ed. Peter Miller, Colin Gordon, and Graham Burchell, 235–250. Hemel Hempstead: Harvester Wheatsheaf.
Pratt, J. 2002. *Punishment and Civilization: Penal Tolerance and Intolerance in Modern Society*. London: Sage.
Pratt, John. 2007. *Penal Populism*. Abingdon: Routledge.

Prebble, J. 1969. *The Highland Clearances*. London: Penguin Books.

Price, V., and P. Neijens. 1997. Opinion Quality in Public Opinion Research. *International Journal of Public Opinion Research* 9 (4): 336–360.

Reiner, R. 2010. *The Politics of the Police*. Oxford: Oxford University Press.

Research, Beaufort. 2004. *Gwent Criminal Justice Board: Public Confidence Survey: Report and Tabulations February–March 2004*. Cardiff: Beaufort Research.

Rix, A., F. Joshua, M. Maguire, and S. Morton. 2009. *Home Office Research Report 28: Improving Public Confidence in the Police: A Review of the Evidence*. London: Home Office.

Robert, Philippe. 1978. *The Extent of Public Information and the Nature of Public Attitudes Towards the Social Control of Crime*. Council of Europe 13th Criminological Research Conference: Public Opinion on Crime and Criminal Justice.

Roberts, Julian V., and Anthony N. Doob. 1989. Sentencing and Public Opinion: Taking False Shadows for True Substances. *Osgoode Hall Law Journal* 27 (3): 491–503.

Roberts, Julian V., and Mike Hough, eds. 2002. *Changing Attitudes to Punishment: Public Opinion, Crime and Justice*. Cullompton: Willan.

———. 2005a. Sentencing Young Offenders: Public opinion in England and Wales. *Criminal Justice* 5 (3): 211–232.

———. 2005b. The State of the Prisons: Exploring Public Knowledge and Opinion. *The Howard Journal* 44 (3): 286–306.

———. 2005c. *Understanding Public Attitudes to Criminal Justice*. Maidenhead: Open University Press.

Roberts, Julian V., Loretta J. Stalans, David Indermaur, and Mike Hough. 2003. *Penal Populism and Public Opinion: Lessons from Five Countries*. Oxford: Oxford University Press.

Rock, Paul. 1979. *Public Opinion and Criminal Legislation*. Council of Europe 13th Criminological Research Conference: Public Opinion on Crime and Criminal Justice.

Rose, N. 1993. Government, Authority and Expertise in Advanced Liberalism. *Economy and Society* 22 (3): 283–300.

Ryan, Mick. 1999. Penal Policy Making Towards the Millennium: Elites and Populists; New Labour and the New Criminology. *International Journal of the Sociology of Law* 27 (1): 1–22.

Salgado, G. 1977. *The Elizabethan Underworld*. Stroud: Sutton.

Salisbury, Heather. 2004. *Public Attitudes to the Criminal Justice System: The Impact of Providing Information to British Crime Survey Respondents*. London: Home Office.

Saward, M. 2003. Enacting Democracy. *Political Studies* 51: 161–179.

Scarman, Lord. 1975. *The Red Lion Square Disorders of 15 June 1974*. London: HMSO, Cmd. 5919.

———. 1981. *The Brixton Disorders 10–12 April 1981*. London: HMSO.
Schneider, Hans Joachim. 1978. *The Influence of Mass Communication Media on Public Opinion on Crime and Criminal Justice*. Council of Europe 13th Criminological Research Conference: Public Opinion on Crime and Criminal Justice.
Shamir, J., and M. Shamir. 2000. *The Anatomy of Public Opinion*. Michigan: University of Michigan Press.
Sharpe, J.A. 1984. *Crime in Early Modern England 1550–1750*. Harlow: Longman.
Shaw, Stephen. 1982. *The People's Justice: A Major Poll of Public Attitudes on Crime and Punishment*. London: Prison Reform Trust.
Singer, Lawrence, and Suzanne Cooper. 2008. *Inform, Persuade and Remind: An Evaluation of a project to Improve Public Confidence in the Criminal Justice System*. London: Ministry of Justice.
Smart, B. 2002. *Michel Foucault*. London: Routledge.
Smith, D. 2007. *Confidence in the Criminal Justice System: What Lies Beneath?* London: Ministry of Justice.
Sparks, R.F. 1981. Surveys of Victimization – An Optimistic Assessment. In *Crime and Justice: An Annual Review of Research*, ed. Norval Morris and Michael H. Tonry, 1–60. Chicago: University of Chicago Press.
Squires, P. 1997. *Criminology and the "Community Safety" Paradigm: Safety, Power and Success and the Limits of the Local*. Belfast: British Criminology Conference Queens University.
Thompson, E.P. 1991. *The Making of the English Working Class*. Harmondsworth: Penguin.
Tonry, M., and D. Green. 2003. Criminology and Public Policy in the USA and UK. In *The Criminological Foundations of Penal Policy*, ed. Lucia Zedner and Andrew Ashworth. Oxford: Oxford University Press.
Turner, Liz. 2008. Public Confidence in the Criminal Justice System: The Impact of a Dominant National-Level Discourse on Research and Practice. *Crime Prevention and Community Safety: An International Journal* 10 (3): 174–189.
Turner, Elizabeth R. 2013. Beyond 'Facts' and 'Values': Rethinking Some Recent Debates About Criminology's Public Role. *British Journal of Criminology* 53 (1): 149–166.
Turner, Liz. 2014. Penal Populism, Deliberative Methods and the Production of 'Public Opinion' on Crime and Punishment. *The Good Society* 23 (1): 87–102.
Turner, Elizabeth R. 2016. Mass Incarceration and Public Opinion on Crime and Justice: From Democratic Theory to Method and Reality. In *Democratic Theory and Mass Incarceration*, ed. Albert W. Dzur, Ian Loader, and Richard Sparks, 213–237. Oxford: Oxford University Press.
Turner, Liz, E. Campbell, A. Dale, and R. Graham. 2009. *Creating a Knowledge-Base of Public Confidence in the Criminal Justice System: Report 5: Final Report on the Empirical Research*. Newcastle upon Tyne: Newcastle University.

Van Dijk, J.M. 1979. *The Extent of Public Information and the Nature of Public Attitudes Towards Crime.* Council of Europe Thirteenth Criminological Research Conference: Public Opinion on Crime and Criminal Justice.

Wacquant, Loic. 2004. Pointers on Pierre Bourdieu and Democratic Politics. *Constellations* 11 (1): 3–15.

———. 2009. *Prisons of Poverty.* Minneapolis: University of Minnesota Press.

Walker, Nigel, and Mike Hough, eds. 1988. *Public Attitudes to Sentencing: Surveys from Five Countries.* Aldershot: Gower.

White, R., and F. Haines. 2008. *Crime and Criminology.* Melbourne: Oxford University Press.

Whitehead, E., and J. Taylor. 2003. Public Confidence in the Criminal Justice System. In *Crime in England and Wales 2001/02: Supplementary Volume*, ed. Claire Flood-Page and Joanna Taylor, 119–134. London: Home Office.

Young, J. 1988. Radical Criminology in Britain: The Emergence of a Competing Paradigm. In *A History of British Criminology*, ed. P. Rock, 159–183. Oxford: Oxford University Press.

———. 1997. Left Realist Criminology: Radical in its Analysis, Realist in its Policy. In *The Oxford Handbook of Criminology*, ed. Rod Morgan, Robert Reiner, and Mike Maguire. Oxford: Oxford University Press.

———. 2003. Winning the Fight Against Crime? New Labour, Populism and Lost Opportunities. In *The New Politics of Crime and Punishment*, ed. R. Matthews and J. Young, 33–47. Cullompton: Willan.

Young, J., and R. Matthews. 2003. New Labour, Crime Control and Social Exclusion. In *The New Politics of Crime and Punishment*, ed. R. Matthews and J. Young, 1–32. Cullompton: Willan.

Index[1]

[1] Note: Page number followed by 'n' refers to notes.

E.R. Turner, *Public Confidence in Criminal Justice*,
Critical Criminological Perspectives,
https://doi.org/10.1007/978-3-319-67897-9

P

R

S

T

V

MIX
Papier aus verantwortungsvollen Quellen
Paper from responsible sources
FSC® C105338

Printed by Books on Demand, Germany